Using Microsoft® Excel 2007

Quick Reference Guide

By Connie Hyslop

Legend

- ⏲ Shortcuts and Timesavers
- ✎ Special Notes
- 💣 Warnings

Trademarks

Company names and product names used in this book have been used for identification purposes only and may be trademarks of the manufacturer. Microsoft® Windows and Excel are registered trademarks of Microsoft Corporation.

COPYRIGHT 2008 Hyslop & Associates, 2 Airport Road, Gilford, NH 03249 (603) 528-6660.

These materials are protected by United States Federal Copyright Law. They may not be copied, electronically or otherwise, without written permission from Hyslop & Associates. They may not be used or paraphrased in the development of other course materials without written permission from Hyslop & Associates. These materials may not be used for instructional purposes without permission from Hyslop & Associates

Revision date: 12/08

ISBN 978-0-578-00833-2

Preface

Welcome to *Microsoft® Excel – Quick Reference Guide*. This book is intended to be a quick reference guide. If you were to attend a class at our school, these are the notes that the average user would write down. We have saved you the time. If we take the notes, you can be assured that the steps are accurate. Our books are intended to be brief and to the point. We have found that most people do not want to work with a cumbersome manual.

We hope you will find our books to be "just the right amount of information" and will want to include our entire series in your library.

Excel 2007

The instructions and screen captures in this edition of our book are intended for people using Microsoft® Excel 2007.

Every effort has been made to supply accurate information. However, Hyslop & Associates does not guarantee the accuracy or completeness of any information and assumes no responsibility for its use.

Table of Contents

Introduction to Spreadsheets 1

Starting and Exiting Excel 1
To start Excel 1
To exit Excel 2

Screen Layout and Options 2
To customize the Quick Access Toolbar 2

Overview of Excel 4
Entering and Editing Data 4
To type data into a cell 5
To edit data in a cell 5
To type the same information into multiple cells 6
To copy information from the above cell 6

Date and Time Shortcuts 6
To insert the current date or time 6
Inserting an automatic date code 6
To change the date format 7

Creating a New Workbook 8
To create a new file 8

Saving a Workbook 8
To save a new workbook 8
To save changes to the current file 9
To save a file using a new name 9
Working in Compatibility Mode 10
To save a file to an earlier version of MS Office 10

Opening and Closing Files 10
To open an existing file 10
Working with the recent files list 11
To change the number of files in the recent files list 11

  To open multiple files at the same time 12
  To switch between open files...12
  To close the current workbook window............................12

Deleting Cell Contents and Formatting 13

  To remove the contents of cells 13
  To remove the format of cells 13
  To remove the contents and formatting of cells..............13

Using Undo 13

  To undo the last action 14

Working with Fill Series 14

  To create a series by copying...15

Formatting Columns 16

  To set column width using an exact setting....................16
  Using the mouse to change column width 16
  To set column width based on the longest entry.....................16
  To set the width of multiple columns 17
  To set the default column width..17
  Adjust column width in Print Preview................................17
  Hiding columns...18
  To redisplay hidden columns 19

Zoom Control...19

  To adjust the percentage 19

Moving Around the Spreadsheet 20

Selecting Cells, Columns and Rows 21

  To select a range of cells..21
  To select nonadjacent cells 21
  To select columns or rows 21
  To select the entire active area of a worksheet 21
  To select a named range...22

Print and Preview a File 22

  To preview the active sheet..22
  To print the active sheet..23
  To print a selected area of a worksheet............................23

To print all active sheets in a workbook 23
To set the print area in a worksheet 24
Previewing and adjusting page breaks 25

Inserting and Deleting Columns or Rows 26

To insert a new column or row 26
To delete a row or column 27

Moving and Copying Text 28

To move information using the Windows Clipboard 28
To move cells using drag and drop 29
To copy information using the Windows Clipboard 29
To copy down a column or across a row 30
To copy information from the above cell 30
To move/copy information from one sheet to another 30
To move/copy information to a different file 31

Formatting Spreadsheets 33

Page Setup 33

To set margins 33
To center a one page report 33
Landscape printing 34
Scale to Fit Page 34
Printing gridlines 35
Print Row & Column headings 35
Using print titles to print headings on every page 36

Headers & Footers 36

To create a header or footer 36
To create a custom header or footer 37

Text formatting – using icons in the Font Group 37

To change the font and size 37
To add bold, italics, and/or underlining 37
Using Borders 38
Changing Font Color 38

Numeric Formatting – Using Icons in the Number Group 39

Controlling dollar signs and comma placement 39
Percent style 39

To change the number of decimal places 39
Custom Formatting 39
To create a custom numeric format 41

Using Icons in the Alignment Group 42

To horizontally align information in a cell 42
To align information vertically in a cell 42
Indenting text in a cell 42
To rotate text on an angle 43
Wrapping text in a cell 43
To center information across multiple cells 44
Using the alignment dialogue box 45
To copy formatting 47

Controlling Page Breaks & Column Titles 48

Freeze titles in the spreadsheet window 48
To insert manual page breaks 49

Building Formulas 51

To write a formula 52
Displaying help for special functions 52
Using the AutoSum icon 53
To add a column or row of numbers 53
To create totals below several columns 54
To create grand totals 54

Absolute Referencing (also known as Absolute Addressing) 54

To write a formula with an absolute reference 55

Using Paste Function 56

Sample Special Function Formulas 56
To use Paste Function 57

PMT 59

ROUND 60

Variations of Round 60

IF 61
IF Statement Examples 62
Lookup Functions 63
   VLOOKUP and HLOOKUP....................................63
Working With Text in a Formula...................................64
Defining and Using Range Names.................................65
   To define a name..65
   To select and go to a named cell or range................65
   To automatically create names from data 66
   Create a reference list of existing range names 66
   To delete a name 67
   To insert a name into a formula 67
Using Auditing Tools..68
   To Trace Precedents..68
   To Trace Dependents 68
   To remove trace arrows 69

Working with Multiple Sheets 71
   To display a sheet..71
   To rename a sheet 71
   Grouping sheets 71
   To copy or move a sheet within the same workbook...............72
   To copy a sheet to a new workbook..........................72
   To insert a sheet between existing sheets 73
   To permanently delete a sheet...................................73
   Change the color of a sheet tab 73
   View multiple sheets in a workbook.........................73
Linking formulas between sheets...................................74
Worksheet Links 75
   To create a link..75
   To update links to unopened books 76

Charts & Drawing Objects 77

Creating a Chart 77

To change an embedded chart to a chart sheet 78
Chart components 79
Activating a chart 80
To resize an embedded chart 80
To move an embedded chart 80

Editing Charts 81

Switch plotted data range from Column to Row 81
To copy new data to an embedded chart 82
To copy new data to a chart sheet 82
To chart multiple ranges 82
Changing the Chart Type 84

Customizing a Chart 85

To change the chart style 85
Choosing from pre-defined Chart Layouts 85

Customizing Chart Layout 86

To add chart and axis titles 86
To customize the chart axes 86
To customize the chart legend 87
To customize the data markers for a series 87
To customize an individual data marker (Data Point) 88
To use a picture in data markers 88
Customizing the Scale 89
To remove the scale 89
To turn the scale back on 89
To format the scale 89
To add values to data markers 90
To customize the gridlines 90
To remove Gridlines 90
To customize the plot area 90
To customize the chart area 91
To adjust the gap width in a column chart 92
To add a text note 93
To add an Arrow or Shape 93

Attaching the Data Table to a Chart 94
    To attach the data table 94
Copying a Chart Sheet 95
    To copy a chart sheet 95
    To change the data range of a chart 95

Templates, Tips & Timesavers 97

Creating a Series 97
    To create a series by dragging 97
    To create a series with the Fill command 98
Creating Custom Lists...99
    To create your own Custom Lists 99
    To use your Custom Lists 99
    Creating a list by importing entries..99
Protecting a Workbook 100
    To protect a worksheet with a password.......................................100
    Protecting cells, sheets, and workbooks from changes..........100
Templates..102
    To create a template 102
    To use a template 103
    To modify a template 103
Using Select Special 104
    To find specific types of cells 104
    Using data validation rules..105
    To compare 2 rows or columns...106
    Replacing formulas with calculated results 106
    To find precedents and dependents of the current cell 107
To print formulas 108
Rearranging Windows 108
    To open a second window displaying the active document...108
    To divide a window into panes 109
    To freeze columns and rows 109
    To print column headings at the top of every page................110

Cell Comments 111
    To create a comment 111
    To delete a comment 111
    To display comments 111
    To print comments 111
    To reformat a comment box 112

Cell Styles 113
    To apply a style 113
    To create a new cell style 114
    To copy styles from another workbook 114

Conditional Formatting 115
    To set conditional formatting 115
    To remove conditional formatting 116

Track Changes 117
    To track changes 117
    To review changes in a document 118

Databases Functions 119

Sorting Information 119

Pivot Tables 120
    To create a PivotTable 121
    Grouping Categories and Show/Hide Details 123
    To group categories 123
    Expanding & Collapsing the Details 124
    To collapse category details 124
    Updating PivotTable Data 125
    PivotTable Formatting Styles 125
    To apply a design 125

Using a List as a Database 126
    To use a list as a database 126
    Using the data form 126
    To use criteria to find records 128

Filtering Records 129
    To turn on the Filter Feature 129

Calculating in a Database 130
    To calculate automatic subtotals and totals in a database 130
Database Functions 132
    To define a criterion range 133

Microsoft® Excel 2007
Introduction to Spreadsheets

Starting and Exiting Excel

To start Excel

- Click the ![start] button on the Windows Taskbar in the bottom left corner of the screen.
- Highlight **All Programs**. Highlight Microsoft® Office and click **Microsoft® Excel.**

or If available, click the shortcut icon on your desktop.

The diagram below describes the parts of the screen. Your screen may not match exactly because many of these items can be customized.

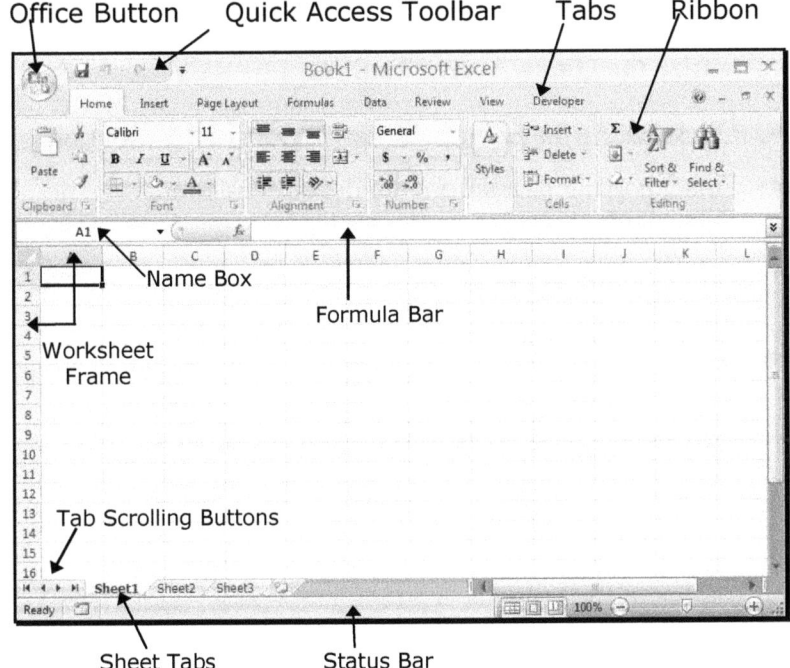

Microsoft® Excel 2007   Quick Reference Guide

To exit Excel

- Save the file (see page 8). Click the Office button in the upper left corner of the screen, choose [X Exit Excel].

Screen Layout and Options

There are many options that control the appearance of the Excel screen. Some screen options can be turned on or off to suit your personal preferences. When you close Excel, screen settings are saved and will appear the same way when you restart the application.

 The *Office Button* in the upper left corner of the screen displays file options, including , Open, Close, Print, Print Preview, Save and Save As.

To the right side of the Office Button is the *Quick Access Toolbar*. The default buttons are Save, Undo and Redo. However you can customize this toolbar and add your favorites. The first thing I added was Print.

To customize the Quick Access Toolbar

- Click the [▼] on the [Customize Quick Access Toolbar] button.
- Select popular items from the list or click More Commands...
- Double-click an item in the **More Commands** list to add it to the toolbar.
- You can change the location of the Quick Access Toolbar to display below the ribbon by selecting this option in the Customize Quick Access Toolbar drop-down.

Microsoft® Excel 2007   Quick Reference Guide

The *Formula Bar* displays information that is being typed into a cell, edited, or that has been previously entered. To toggle the formula bar on/off, click the **View** tab on the ribbon and select or deselect the ☑ Formula Bar check box.

The *Frame* displays column letters across the top and row numbers down the left side of the worksheet window.

The *Vertical Scroll Bar* appears on the right side of the window and is used to scroll up/down in a worksheet.

The *Horizontal Scroll Bar* appears below the spreadsheet area. At the beginning of the scroll bar are *sheet tabs* that show the names of worksheets in the workbook. The size of the horizontal scroll bar can be changed to enlarge the area to view sheet tabs. Position the mouse on the vertical bar at the beginning of the scroll bar. The mouse pointer will change to a double vertical bar with arrows pointing in both directions. Click and drag to resize the scroll bar.

The *Status Bar* and *Zoom* buttons appear below the horizontal scroll bar. This bar displays the status of the worksheet, including the current Zoom, Page Number, whether Caps Lock or Num Lock is on and much more. To customize what you see on the Status Bar, right-click on the bar and select or deselect features.

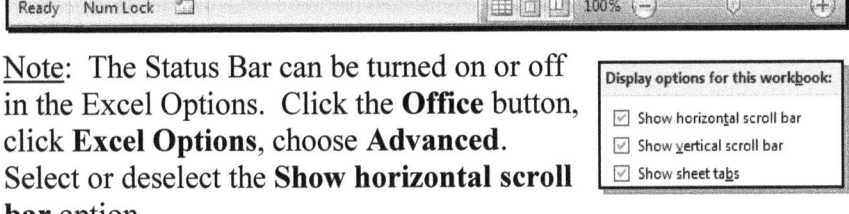

Note: The Status Bar can be turned on or off in the Excel Options. Click the **Office** button, click **Excel Options**, choose **Advanced**. Select or deselect the **Show horizontal scroll bar** option.

Microsoft® Excel 2007 — Quick Reference Guide

Overview of Excel

An Excel file is a *workbook* that consists of one or more *worksheets*. If a workbook includes multiple sheets for different parts of a report or project, the sheet name displays on *sheet tabs* at the bottom of the workbook window. A worksheet is organized into columns and rows and the intersection of a column/row is called a *cell*. The current cell is known as the active cell or *cell address*. Here are a few numbers to remember:

- A new workbook consists of 3 sheets and can be increased to 255 sheets.

- A sheet contains 16,384 columns and 1,048,576 rows. This is 17,179,869,184 cells and approximately 40,628,331 pages *on each sheet*.

- ✎ If you save a file in Compatibility Mode, a sheet is limited to 256 columns by 65,536 rows. For more information on saving in compatibility mode, see page 10.

Entering and Editing Data

There are three basic types of information that can be typed into a cell.

- A *Text Constant* can include letters, number and symbols. Numbers entered with text cannot be calculated. Text aligns on the left by default.

- Numbers are entered as *Values* that can be used in a formula to perform calculations. Values may contain numbers, + - $ % and ( ). Numbers automatically align on the right.

- *Formulas* are used to perform calculations. A formula starts with an equal [=] and may include numbers and mathematical operators. For example, add [+], subtract [-], multiply [*] and divide [/].

Microsoft® Excel 2007　　　　Quick Reference Guide

To type data into a cell

- Click in the middle of a cell. The mouse pointer should be a fat cross.

- Type the information and

    press [ENTER] to move down a cell

    [TAB] to move to the right a cell

    [SHIFT] [TAB] to move to the left a cell

    or click the checkmark ✓ on the formula bar to enter the information without advancing to the next cell.

    The ✗ is used to cancel without changing the information in the current cell.

To edit data in a cell

There are 4 different ways to edit data in a cell.

- Click on the cell.

    1. Retype the information and press [ENTER].

    2. Click on the formula bar and type to insert new characters. Press [DELETE] to remove characters to the right of the insertion point and [BACKSPACE] to remove characters to the left of the insertion point. Press [ENTER] when revisions are complete.

    3. Press [F2]

    4. Double-click the cell. Press [ENTER] when revisions are complete.

Microsoft® Excel 2007   Quick Reference Guide

To type the same information into multiple cells

- Select a block of cells by dragging with the mouse.
- Type the information and press [CTRL][ENTER].

To copy information from the above cell

- Hold [CTRL] and press the ' (apostrophe) key.

Date and Time Shortcuts

Excel includes a couple of ways to enter today's date. You can use a keyboard shortcut to quickly enter the current date or you can write a formula that will automatically update when you open the file.

To insert the current date or time

- Click on a cell and press [CTRL][;] (semicolon) to insert the current date.
- Click on a cell and press [CTRL][SHIFT][:] (colon) to insert the current time.

✎ The keyboard shortcuts shown above will <u>not</u> automatically update in the future.

Inserting an automatic date code

A date code will update automatically when you print the workbook. To create a date formula:

- Click on the cell.
- Type the formula =TODAY( ) and press [ENTER]. Do not include any spaces in the formula. If you have not previously formatted the cell, the date will display in the format 1/22/09.

Microsoft® Excel 2007　　　　Quick Reference Guide

Or Type the formula =NOW( ) and press [ENTER]. Do not include any spaces in the formula. If you have not previously formatted the cell, the date will display in the format 1/22/2009 9:39 PM.

Type	Displays As
=NOW()	7/19/2007 12:18
=TODAY()	7/19/2007

To change the date format

- Right-click on the date in the cell and choose **Format Cells**. On the **Number** folder tab, click **Date** and choose the desired format.

Microsoft® Excel 2007 — Quick Reference Guide

Creating a New Workbook

When you first start Excel, a new workbook displays automatically. When you close the current book, the worksheet window disappears.

To create a new file

- Click the **Office** button.
- Click **New**.
- Choose the **Blank Workbook** template and click the **Create** command button.

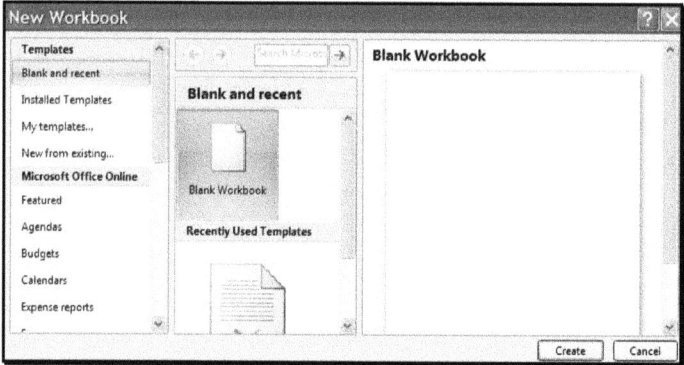

- Or press [CTRL][N] if you prefer keyboard shortcuts.

Saving a Workbook

When a file is saved for the first time a name must be assigned using the *Save As* menu. If a file has previously been saved, use the *Save* option to save the current changes. If you want to save an existing workbook as a new file, use *Save As*.

To save a new workbook

- Click the **Office** button.
- Highlight **Save As**.
- Click **Excel Workbook** to save the file in 2007 format or choose Excel 97-2003 to save the file in compatibility mode.

Microsoft® Excel 2007   Quick Reference Guide

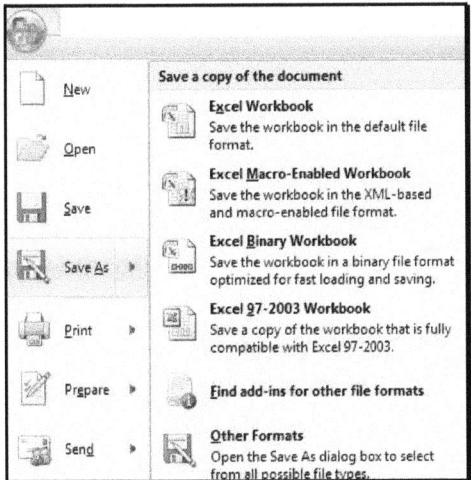

- Type a name for the file. A filename can include letters, numbers and spaces. Do not use punctuation or symbols.
- Choose the drive or folder you want to save the file in – example: the My Documents folder.
- Click the **Save** command button

To save changes to the current file

- Click the **Office** button.
- Click **Save**.

- Press [CTRL][S] or click the Save icon on the Quick Access Toolbar.

To save a file using a new name

If you open an existing file and save it under a new name, Excel will create a copy of the file.

- Click the **Office** button.
- Highlight **Save As**. Choose the file format you want.
- Type a new filename. Do not use punctuation or symbols.
- Click the **Save** command button.

Microsoft® Excel 2007   Quick Reference Guide

Working in Compatibility Mode

MS Office 2007 saves documents in a new format (XML) which is not compatible with prior versions. If you save your file in the 97-2003 format, this is considered Compatibility Mode and the file can be read by all versions of Office. However, if you save in compatibility mode, some new features in Excel 2007 may not be available.

To save a file to an earlier version of MS Office

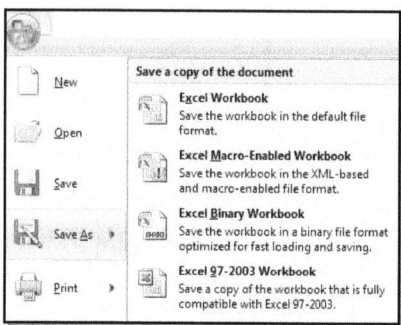

- Click the **Office** button in the upper left corner of the screen.
- Highlight **Save As**.
- Choose the Excel 97-2003 Workbook format.

✎ You can set the default format to the compatibility mode for all new files you create and save. Click the **Office** button and click **Excel Options**. Click the **Save** category on the left side of the screen. Click the drop-down on **Save Files in this Format** and choose the **Excel 97-2003 Workbook** setting.

Opening and Closing Files

To open an existing file

- Click the **Office** button.
- Choose **Open**.
- Highlight the filename and click the **Open** button *or* Double-click the filename.

Microsoft® Excel 2007   Quick Reference Guide

- If the file is not displayed in the current folder, double-click the folder icon to switch folders. If the file resides on a different drive, drop-down the **Look In** list and click the appropriate drive letter.

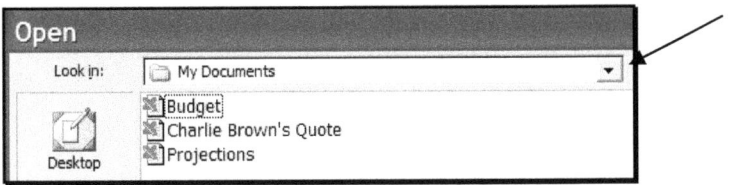

🕐 To access the Open dialog box quickly, press [CTRL][O].

Working with the recent files list

A list of the 17 most recently used files displays when you click the Office **button**. Click the filename to open the file. You can change the option for recent files to display up to 50 files. If you have files you want to ensure stay in the recent files list, you can pin the file to the list.

To pin a file to the recent files list

- Click the **Office** button.

- Click the 📌 push pin to the right of the filename. Click the 📌 push pin again to unpin the file from the list.

To change the number of files in the recent files list

- Click the **Office** button.

- Click the 🔘 Excel Options button.

- Click the **Advanced** category on the left. Scroll down to the **Display** section.

- Set your preference for the number of files, maximum of 50.

- 11 -

Microsoft® Excel 2007   Quick Reference Guide

To open multiple files at the same time

- Click the **Office** button. Choose **Open.**
- Click the first filename you want to open
- Hold the [CTRL] key and click each additional filename.
- Click the **Open** command button.

To switch between open files

- Click the **Switch Windows** button on the **View** tab and select a file from the list.
- 🕐 Press [CTRL][F6] repeatedly to cycle through open files within the same application. Open files also appear on the Windows Taskbar at the bottom of the screen. Click a button to switch files.

To close the current workbook window

- Save the file.
- Click the **Office** button.
- Choose **Close.**
- 🕐 Click the file Close box ⊠ to quickly close the open window or press [CTRL][W].

Microsoft® Excel 2007   Quick Reference Guide

Deleting Cell Contents and Formatting

To remove the contents of cells

- Select the cells to be cleared.
- Click the **Clear** button on the **Home** tab. Choose **Clear Contents**.

Or Select the cells and press [DELETE]. The cell format is not removed.

To remove the format of cells

- Select the cells.
- Click the **Clear** button on the **Home** tab. Choose **Clear Formats**. The cell format returns to the General format.

To remove the contents and formatting of cells

- Select the cells.
- Click the **Clear** button on the **Home** tab. Choose **Clear All**. The cell format returns to the General format.

Using Undo

If you make a mistake or get in trouble, the Undo function will reverse your most recent actions. Office applications can remember up to 100 actions. If you click Undo too many times, you can use Redo to Undo the Undo.

- 13 -

Microsoft® Excel 2007   Quick Reference Guide

To undo the last action

- Click the **Undo** icon on the Quick Access Toolbar. Use the down arrow on the undo icon to display a list of items in the undo buffer.

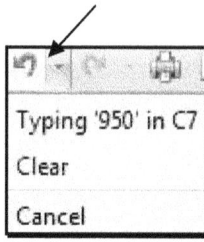

✎ If you want to reverse the undo, click the **Redo** button.

Working with Fill Series

The black dot in the lower right corner of the active cell is known as the *fill handle*. The fill handle is used to copy information down a column or across a row. If the information in the cell appears to be part of a series, Excel will continue the series rather than copy. This can be used to fill the days of the week or months of the year. If the cell contains a combination of letters and numbers, Excel will assume the text should remain constant but the number should automatically increment.
For example:

Original cell	Copies as
Sunday	Monday, Tuesday, Wednesday, etc.
January	February, March, April, etc.
1st Qtr	2nd Qtr, 3rd Qtr, 4th Qtr
Check #1001	Check #1002, Check #1003, etc.

Microsoft® Excel 2007   Quick Reference Guide

To create a series by copying

- Select the cell to copy.

- Position the mouse pointer on the *fill handle* in the lower right corner of the cell. Be sure the shape of the mouse pointer is a thin black cross.

- Drag the fill handle down or across to select the cells to copy to.

- A smart tag will display when you use the fill handle. Hover over the tag and click the drop-down arrow to display fill choices.

Here are examples:

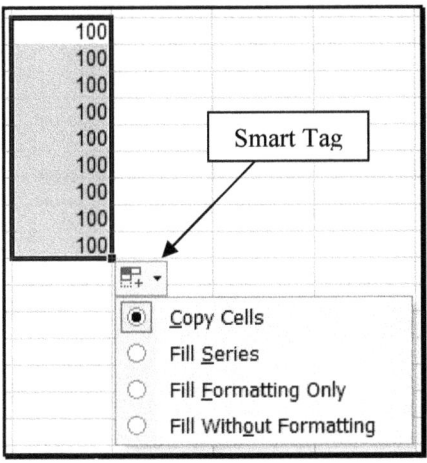
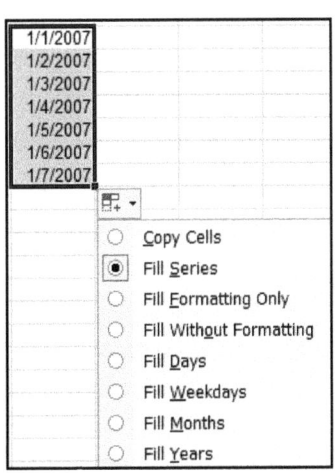

- 15 -

Microsoft® Excel 2007　　　Quick Reference Guide

Formatting Columns

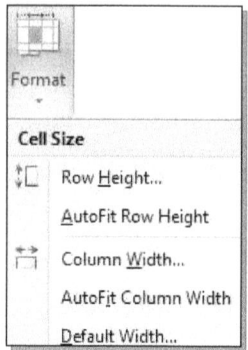

If a column is not wide enough to display the contents of the cell, text will overlap into the next cell if it is blank. If the cell contains a value with formatting that is too wide for the cell, a series of ##### will display.

Widen the column to correct this problem.

To set column width using an exact setting

- Position the pointer anywhere in the column or select multiple columns.

- On the **Home** tab, click the **Format** button. Click **Column Width**. Specify an exact size and click OK.

Using the mouse to change column width

- Position the mouse pointer on the column divider to the right of the column letter. The mouse pointer will change to a vertical line with arrows pointing in both directions.

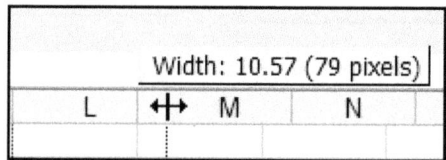

- Drag the column divider to the new width. A ScreenTip box displays the column width while you are holding the mouse button down.

To set column width based on the longest entry

- Double-click on the column divider to the right of the column letter.

Microsoft® Excel 2007   Quick Reference Guide

- ✎ To set the column width based on a selected range of cells, highlight the cells. On the **Home** tab, click the **Format** button and choose **AutoFit Column Width**.

To set the width of <u>multiple</u> columns

- Select multiple columns.
- Click and drag any column divider in the highlighted area to set the columns to the *same* width
- or Select columns, double-click the column divider to set each of the selected columns to the best fit. Columns will *not* be the same width.

To set the default column width

The Standard Width option controls the width of all columns in the <u>current</u> sheet. The default width is 8.43. This does not affect columns that have been set individually. To specify a new setting:

- On the **Home** tab, click the **Format** button. Click **Default Width**.
- Type a setting for all columns in the current sheet and click OK.

Adjust column width in Print Preview

If you display a spreadsheet in Print Preview and decide at the last minute that you want to adjust the width of a column you can display margin and column guides. This is useful for adjusting one column at a time and you want to see whether the change effects where the page break falls.

- In the Print Preview screen, click the [Show Margins] checkbox at the top of the screen. Column dividers ┬ will display at the top of the page.

Microsoft® Excel 2007   Quick Reference Guide

- Position the mouse pointer on the ▼. Click and drag the divider to change the width.
- Click the [✓ Show Margins] button again to hide the dividers.

Hiding columns

If you hide a column or row, it will not print. Sometimes you need to refer to information in a spreadsheet as you are working but you do not want the information to print. For example, you may want to write a formula that calculates your employees average salary but you do not want to show how much everyone earns on the spreadsheet. When a column is hidden, its' column letter will not display in the spreadsheet window. To hide column(s)

- Select the column(s).
- Click the **Format** button on the **Home** tab.
- Highlight **Hide & Unhide** and click **Hide Columns**.

	A	D	E
1	THE CORNER GARDENS		
2	Greenhouse Inventory		
3			
4			
5			
6	Annual Flowers	Total Packs	
7	Asters	350	
8	Alyssum	390	
9	Dahlias	310	

- Or *Right*-click on the column letter and choose Hide.
- Or Drag the column divider to the left until the column *completely* disappears

Microsoft® Excel 2007   Quick Reference Guide

To redisplay hidden columns

- Click and drag to select the columns on either side of the hidden one(s)
- Click the **Format** button on the **Home** tab.
- Highlight **Hide & Unhide** and click **Unhide Columns**.

Or *Right*-click on the column letter and choose Unhide.

Zoom Control

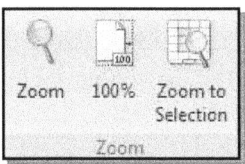

The Zoom setting controls how much you see on the screen at one time in Excel. Zoom *does not* affect the size of the text when you print.

To adjust the percentage

- Click the **Zoom** button on the **Home** tab. Choose a percentage and click OK.

Or click the + and – on the zoom bar at the bottom right corner of the screen.

✎ Highlight multiple columns and click the **Zoom to Selection** button on the **View** tab to adjust the percentage for specific columns. Excel calculates the percentage you need for the selected columns to fit perfectly on the screen.

Microsoft® Excel 2007　　　Quick Reference Guide

Moving Around the Spreadsheet

To move from one area to another in a spreadsheet, use the following options:

Next or previous cell	[TAB] or [SHIFT][TAB] or ← →
Up or down one cell	↑ ↓
Go To a specific cell	Click the cell *or*
	Press [CTRL][G], type the cell address and press [ENTER]
First or last active cell in the current sheet	[CTRL][HOME] or [CTRL][END]
Beginning or end of current row	[HOME] or [END] →
Boundary between an empty and a nonempty cell	[CTRL] → or [CTRL] ←
Screen Up or Screen Down	[PGUP] or [PGDN]
	or click the vertical scroll bar above or below the scroll box
Screen Left or Screen Right	[ALT][PGUP] or [ALT][PGDN]
	or
	click the horizontal scroll bar on the left or right side of the scroll box.
Next or Previous Sheet	Click the sheet tab at the bottom of the screen *or* press [CTRL][PGUP] or [CTRL][PGDN]

Microsoft® Excel 2007   Quick Reference Guide

Selecting Cells, Columns and Rows

To work with a specific part of a worksheet, cells must be selected. Selected cells can be formatted, deleted, moved, copied, sorted or printed.

To select a range of cells

- Position the mouse pointer in the middle of the first cell. Be sure the pointer is shaped like a fat cross. Click and drag the mouse across the cells.

or Hold [SHIFT] and press → or ↓ cursor movement keys.

or Click on the first cell, hold [SHIFT] down, click on the last cell.

☼ [CTRL][*] selects all adjacent cells until a blank cell is detected. Note: Use the * on the numeric keypad or [CTRL][SHIFT][8]

To select nonadjacent cells

- Click the first cell to be selected. Hold the [CTRL] key and click additional cells in the worksheet.

✎ When you select nonadjacent cells, you can delete or format the cells. Move and copy cannot be executed on nonadjacent cells.

To select columns or rows

- Click the column letter above the column, or the row number to the left of the row.

or Drag across several column letters or row numbers.

☼ Press [CTRL][SPACE] to select the current column or [SHIFT][SPACE] to select the current row.

To select the entire active area of a worksheet

- Click on the first cell. Hold [SHIFT] and press [CTRL][END].

Microsoft® Excel 2007   Quick Reference Guide

To select a named range

- Click the drop-down arrow on the Name Box and select the name.

Print and Preview a File

To preview the active sheet

- Click the **Office** button, highlight **Print** and choose **Print Preview**.
- The Print Preview icon can be added to the Quick Access toolbar. See page 2 for instructions.

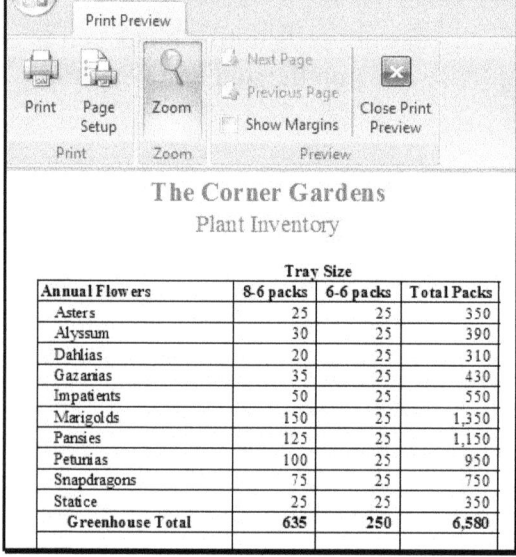

- Click on the page to toggle between a full-page view and a magnified view of the page.
- Use the vertical scroll bar or press [PAGEUP] and [PAGEDOWN] to move through the file.
- Click the **Close Print Preview** button to return to the worksheet window.

Microsoft® Excel 2007   Quick Reference Guide

To print the active sheet

- From the worksheet area, click the **Office** button, highlight **Print** and click **Quick Print**.
- The Quick Print icon can be added to the Quick Access Toolbar. See page 2 for instructions.

To print a selected area of a worksheet

- Highlight the information to be printed.
- Click the **Office** button, highlight **Print** and click **Print**.

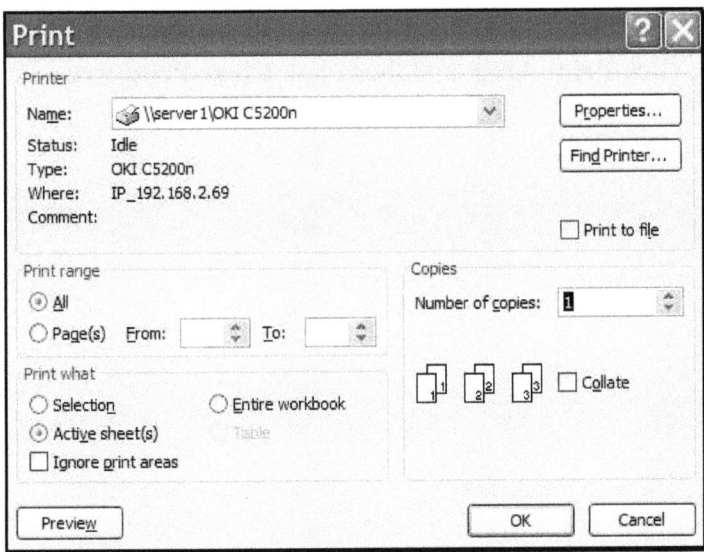

- In the **Print What** box choose **Selection**. Click OK.

To print all active sheets in a workbook

- Click the **Office** button, highlight **Print** and choose **Print**.
- In the **Print What** box choose **Entire Workbook** and click OK.

Microsoft® Excel 2007　　　Quick Reference Guide

To set the print area in a worksheet

If you set a print area, any data outside the selected area will not print. This is useful if you always print the same part of a sheet. To set the area:

- Highlight the cells to be printed.
- On the **Page Layout** tab, click **Print Area**, and then click **Set Print Area**.

✎ The entire worksheet will not print until you clear the print area. To remove the print area, click the **Page Layout** tab, click **Print Area**, and then click **Clear Print Area**.

Microsoft® Excel 2007   Quick Reference Guide

Previewing and adjusting page breaks

From the Print Preview screen you can view the location of page breaks and adjust them to control where pages break between rows or columns. To view and adjust breaks:

- On the **View** tab, click the **Page Break Preview** button.

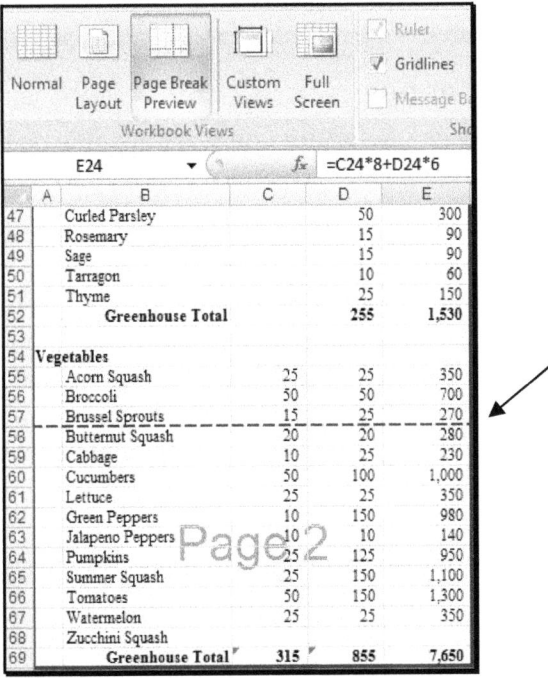

- Position the mouse pointer on the blue line. The pointer will change to a 2 headed arrow.

- Drag to move the page break to a new location. The page will always break in the new location and will not be adjusted if rows are inserted or deleted on a sheet.

- To return the screen to normal, click the **Normal** button on the **View** tab.

- 25 -

Microsoft® Excel 2007   Quick Reference Guide

Inserting and Deleting Columns or Rows

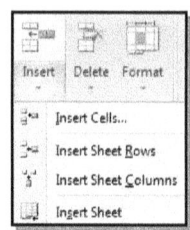

When you build a spreadsheet you do not always think of everything in the beginning. If you insert a new row in the middle of the sheet, it will be inserted above the row you have selected. When you insert a new column, it will appear in front of the current column.

To insert a new column or row

- Select the column or row where you want the new one to appear.

- On the **Home** tab, click the **Insert** button and choose **Insert Sheet Rows** or **Insert Sheet Columns**.
  Note: The Insert button has 2 parts. If you click the top part of the button, Excel will automatically insert based on the highlighted area. For example, if a row is highlighted, Excel will insert a new row. If you click on the bottom part of the button, options will display to insert a cell, column, row or sheet.

- To insert more than one row or column you can highlight multiple rows or columns and then insert rows or columns as described above.

- You can also press [CTRL][+] to add columns/rows or *Right*-click the mouse on the selected row or column and choose **Insert**.

Microsoft® Excel 2007   **Quick Reference Guide**

To delete a row or column

- Select the row(s) or column(s) to be deleted.
- On the **Home** tab, click the **Delete** button or press [CTRL][-].
  Note: The Delete button has 2 parts. If you click the top part of the button, Excel will automatically delete based on the highlighted area. For example, if a row is highlighted, Excel will delete a row. If you click on the bottom part of the button, options will display to delete a cell, column, row or sheet.
- *Right*-click the mouse on the selected row or column and choose **Delete**.

Microsoft® Excel 2007　　　Quick Reference Guide

Moving and Copying Text

Information in a worksheet can be moved or copied using the Windows Clipboard or by dragging and dropping. When the clipboard is used information can be pasted multiple times or can be copied to a different sheet in the workbook. The clipboard can also be used to copy information from one file to another. Drag and drop is limited to the same worksheet and the information is not retained to be copied multiple times.

To move information using the Windows Clipboard

* Select the information to be moved.

* Click the **Cut** button on the **Home** tab or press [CTRL][X]. The information is placed in the Windows clipboard and a flashing marquee appears around the range.

* Position the pointer where the information should be placed. Click the **Paste** button on the **Home** tab or press [CTRL][V]. The data is removed from the original location. The marquee will continue to flash so that information can be pasted multiple times. Press [ESC] to clear the marquee.

⏲ You can right click on selected cells and choose Cut and Paste from the shortcut menu.

✎ If you press [ENTER] after choosing Cut, the information will be pasted in the current location and cleared from the Windows clipboard. Information that has been pasted using [ENTER] can not be pasted multiple times.

Microsoft® Excel 2007   Quick Reference Guide

To move cells using drag and drop

- Select the cells to move.
- Position the mouse pointer on any edge of the selected area. The mouse pointer will change to a 4 headed arrow.

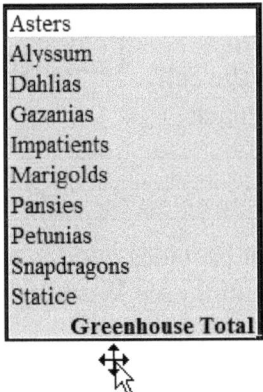

- Drag the selected area to its new position.
- If this will overwrite existing cells, click **OK** to confirm the move.

To copy information using the Windows Clipboard

- Select the information to be moved.
- Click the **Copy** button on the **Home** tab or press [CTRL][C]. The information is placed in the Windows clipboard and a flashing marquee appears around the range.
- Position the pointer where the information should be placed. Click the **Paste** button on the **Home** tab or press [CTRL][V]. The data remains in the original location. The marquee will continue to flash so that information can be pasted multiple times. Press [ESC] to clear the marquee.
- ☺ You can right click on selected cells and choose Copy and Paste from the shortcut menu.
- ✎ If you press [ENTER] after choosing Copy, the information will be pasted in the current location and cleared from the

Microsoft® Excel 2007   Quick Reference Guide

Windows clipboard. Information that has been pasted using [ENTER] can not be pasted multiple times.

To copy down a column or across a row

- Highlight the cell(s) to copy.

- Position the mouse pointer on the *fill handle* in the lower right corner of the cell. Be sure the pointer shape is a thin black cross.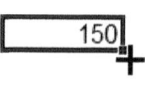

- Drag the fill handle down or across to select the cells to copy to. A smart tag will display that provides options to copy or fill as a series. For more information, see Working with Fill Series on page 14.

- When formulas are copied, the copies adjust to the new position of each formula automatically. For more information on Relative and Absolute Referencing, see page 54 for more information.

To copy information from the above cell

- Hold [CTRL] and press the ' (apostrophe) key.

To move/copy information from one sheet to another

- Select the information to be moved or copied.

- Click the **Cut** or **Copy** button on the **Home** tab. The information is placed in the Windows clipboard and a flashing marquee appears around the range.

- Switch to the new sheet by clicking the sheet tab. Position the pointer where the information should be placed. Click the **Paste** button on the **Home** tab or press [CTRL][V].

- 30 -

Microsoft® Excel 2007   Quick Reference Guide

To move/copy information to a different file

- Select the information to be moved or copied.

- Click the **Cut** or **Copy** button on the **Home** tab. The information is placed in the Windows clipboard and a flashing marquee appears around the range.

- Open the target file.

- Position the pointer where the data should be placed and press [ENTER] or click the **Paste** button on the **Home** tab.

Formatting Spreadsheets

Page Setup

The Page Layout tab includes features to control how the worksheet page prints.

To set margins

- Click the **Page Layout** tab. Click the **Margins** button.

- Click one of the predefined margin settings – Normal, Wide or Narrow.

- Or click the **Custom Margins** option and change the margin settings, click OK.

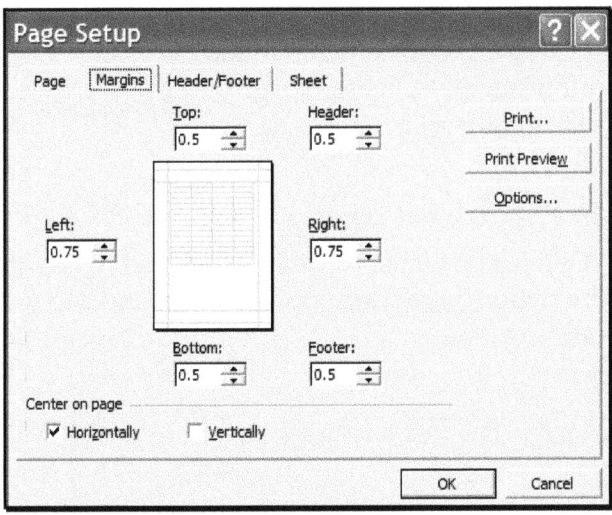

To center a one page report

- To center the page horizontally and/or vertically within the margins, click the **Page Layout** tab on the ribbon. Click the **Margins** button and choose **Custom Margins**.

- On the **Margins** folder tab, click the check box to select **Center on Page Horizontally** and/or **Vertically**

Microsoft® Excel 2007 Quick Reference Guide

Landscape printing

- To change to page orientation to landscape (sideways), click the **Page Layout** tab on the ribbon.

- Click the **Orientation** button. Choose **Landscape**.

✎ All pages on the current sheet will print landscape. Each sheet in a workbook can have a different orientation.

Scale to Fit Page

When you preview a spreadsheet you may find that you have too many columns to fit on the page. Use the Scale to Fit Page option to make a wide report fit to one page wide by many pages tall.

- To force a spreadsheet to fit on a page, click the **Page Layout** tab on the ribbon. Click the **Width** button in the **Scale to Fit** group. Choose 1 page or specify the appropriate number of pages wide.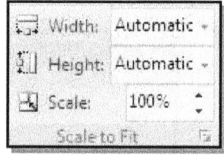

Or Click the **Page Layout** tab on the ribbon. Click the **Page Setup** dialogue box launcher . In the Scaling group click the **Fit to** option button and specify how many pages wide by pages tall.

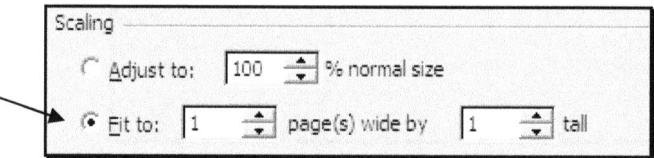

✎ If you specify how many pages wide and delete the setting for tall, Excel will automatically calculate how many pages tall (and visa versa).

Microsoft® Excel 2007   Quick Reference Guide

Printing gridlines

- To print gridlines around all active cells in a worksheet, click the **Page Layout** tab. In the **Sheet Options** group, click the **Print** check box under **Gridlines**.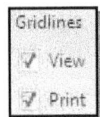

- ✎ This features prints gridlines around ALL cells in the current sheet. To print lines around a selected area only, do not use the Gridline feature. Highlight the range and use the Borders icon on the **Home** tab. For more information on borders, see page 38.

Print Row & Column headings

The Print Row & Column headings feature will print the worksheet frame that includes column letters and row numbers. This is useful if you need a reference sheet and want to easily identify cells at a glance.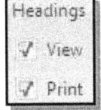

To include row numbers or column letters when you print the file:

- Click the **Page Layout** tab. In the **Sheet Options** group, select the **Print** check box under **Headings**.

	A	B	C	D	E
1		THE CORNER GARDENS			
2		Greenhouse Inventory			
3					
4			Tray Size		
5		Annual Flowers	8-6 packs	6-6 packs	Total Packs
6		Asters	25	25	350
7		Alyssum	30	25	390
8		Dahlias	20	25	310
9		Gazanias	35	25	430
10		Impatients	50	25	550
11		Marigolds	150	25	1,350
12		Pansies	125	25	1,150
13		Petunias	100	25	950
14		Snapdragons	75	25	750
15		Statice	25	25	350
16		Greenhouse Total	635	250	6,580

Microsoft® Excel 2007   Quick Reference Guide

Using print titles to print headings on every page

If you want to print column heading at the top of each printed page, use the Print Titles feature.

- Click the **Page Layout** tab and click the **Print Titles** button.

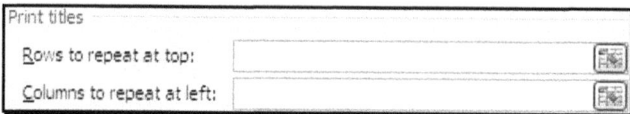

- Set **Rows to repeat at top** to the rows that you want printed first on every page or use the  to display the spreadsheet window and select the rows.

- Set **Columns to repeat at left** to the columns that you want printed at the left margin on every page.

✎ The Columns/Rows to Repeat feature is not available if you go to Page Setup from the Print Preview Screen. Close Print Preview and use the Print Titles button on the Page Layout tab.

Headers & Footers

To create a header or footer

- Click the **Insert** tab on the ribbon.

- Click the **Header &Footer** button.
  This switches the spreadsheet to Page Layout view and places the insertion point in the header window. The Header & Footer Design tab appears on the ribbon. The header & footer windows include 3 parts – information you want printed at the left margin, in the center of the page or at the right margin.

- To choose from preformatted headers & footers, click the Header or Footer button at the beginning of the Header & Footer Design tab. Sample headers include the company name, user name,

- 36 -

Microsoft® Excel 2007   Quick Reference Guide

page number, filename, sheet name and many more. Click one to select it and automatically format the header or footer. Any part of the header or footer can be customized.

To create a custom header or footer

- Follow the steps in the previous section to open the header or footer window. Type the header information or click the **Go to Footer** button on the Header & Footer Design tab.

- Type text or insert codes by clicking one of the following buttons in the Header & Footer Elements group.

- Click any cell in the spreadsheet to continue working. To return to the Normal view, click the **View** tab on the ribbon and click the **Normal** button.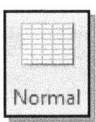

Text formatting – using icons in the Font Group

The **Font** group on the **Home** tab includes buttons used to format the appearance of text and numbers.

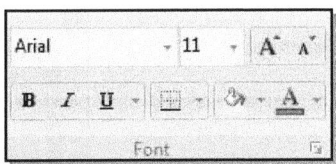

To change the font and size

- Select the cell(s) to be formatted.

- Click the drop-down arrow on the Font list and click to select a font.

- Click the drop-down arrow on the Font Size and click to select a size.

To add bold, italics, and/or underlining

- Select the cell(s) to be formatted.

- 37 -

Microsoft® Excel 2007   Quick Reference Guide

- Click the Bold, Italic, and/or Underline icons  to add or remove attributes.

Using Borders

The gridline option in page setup applies lines to all cells in a spreadsheet. If you want to apply lines/borders to part of a sheet, use the borders icon on the **Home** tab.

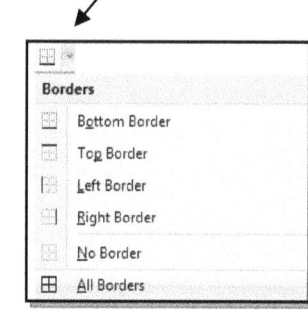

- Select a range of cells. On the **Home** tab, click the drop-down arrow on the **Borders** icon in the font group.

- Choose a border style.

Changing Font Color

- To change the font color, select cells.

- On the **Home** tab, click the drop-down arrow on the Font Color button.

- Click a color.

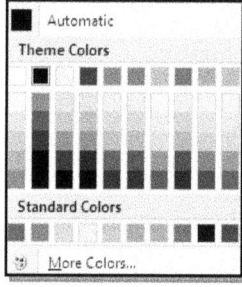

To fill a cell with color or shading

- Select cells.

- On the **Home** tab, click the drop-down arrow on the **Fill Color** button.

- Choose a color.

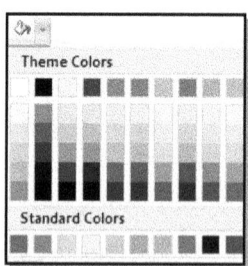

Microsoft® Excel 2007 — Quick Reference Guide

Numeric Formatting – Using Icons in the Number Group

The number format of all cells in a new spreadsheet are set to General format. To change the appearance of numbers, select the cells and choose from the following button in the **Number** group on the **Home** tab.

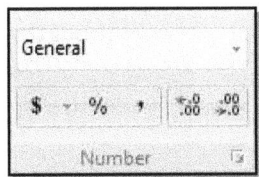

Controlling dollar signs and comma placement

- Click the [$] **Accounting Number Format** icon to add a currency symbol, comma separators, parentheses around negative numbers, and 2 decimal places.

- Click the [,] **Comma Style** icon to add comma separators, parentheses around negative numbers, and 2 decimal places.

Percent style

- Click the [%] **Percent Style** icon to convert the number to a percentage.

To change the number of decimal places

- Click the **Increase Decimal** icon to add a decimal place.

- or Click the **Decrease Decimal** icon to remove a decimal place.

- Click the drop-down arrow on the [General] **General** button to choose from a list of common number formats.

Custom Formatting

In addition to the number formatting buttons on the Home tab, the Format Cells Number dialogue box includes more formatting options.

Microsoft® Excel 2007   Quick Reference Guide

- Select the cell(s).
- Click the ⊞ dialogue box launcher in the **Number** group on the **Home** tab.

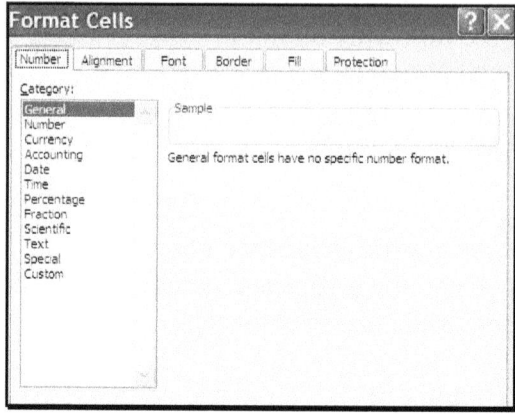

Refer to the diagram below for specific formats.

General	Number	Currency	Accounting	Comma
5	5.00	$5.00	$ 5.00	5.00
5.5	5.50	$5.50	$ 5.50	5.50
5.55	5.55	$5.55	$ 5.55	5.55
5000	5000.00	$5,000.00	$ 5,000.00	5,000.00
-50	-50.00	-$50.00	$ (50.00)	(50.00)
0	0.00	$0.00	$ -	-

	Special		
ZipCode	Phone #	Soc Sec #	Account #
03246	(603) 528-6660	001-46-5493	000000123
03253	(603) 528-6732	003-44-0378	000123456
03301	(978) 356-1234	002-76-0203	000000123
03220	(603) 267-6179	002-76-4224	123456789

Microsoft® Excel 2007 — Quick Reference Guide

To create a custom numeric format

- On the **Home** tab click the ▣ dialogue box launcher in the **Number** group.
- Choose **Custom**.
- Select the Format Code that is closest to the one you want to create. Edit the format in the **Type** box displayed at the top of the menu. Use the following options to control the Code Format:

0	digit displays; if there is no digit for this position, a 0 displays.
#	digit displays; if there is no digit for this position, nothing displays.
,	comma separators appear to separate thousands, millions, etc.
.	decimal point always displays.
$	dollar sign always displays.
;	negative numbers receive the picture given after the semicolon
[red]	negative numbers display in red.
%	percent sign always displays

Microsoft® Excel 2007 — Quick Reference Guide

Using Icons in the Alignment Group

The **Alignment** group on the **Home** tab includes icons to control and text and numeric alignment of cells.

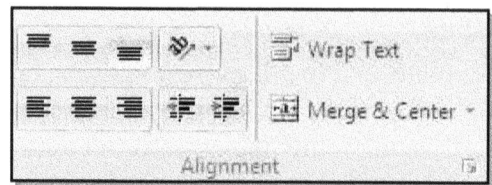

To horizontally align information in a cell

- Select the cell(s) to be aligned.

- Click one of the alignment tools in the **Alignment** group on the **Home** tab – Left, Center or Right.

To align information vertically in a cell

When the height of a cell is taller than the amount of information in the cell, the data lines up at the bottom of the cell. To change the vertical alignment:

- Select the cells.

- Click the [icon] **Top Align**, **Middle Align** or **Bottom Align** button in the Alignment group.

Indenting text in a cell

The indent feature is used to indent text in a cell rather than use separate columns. To indent text:

- Select the cell(s).

- Click the **Increase Indent** button in the **Alignment** group on the **Home** tab. Click the Increase Indent button multiple times to increase the level of indent.

Microsoft® Excel 2007   Quick Reference Guide

✎ Use the **Decrease Indent** button to move text back to the left side of the cell.

To rotate text on an angle

♦ Select cells. On the **Home** tab, click the [icon] **Orientation** button.

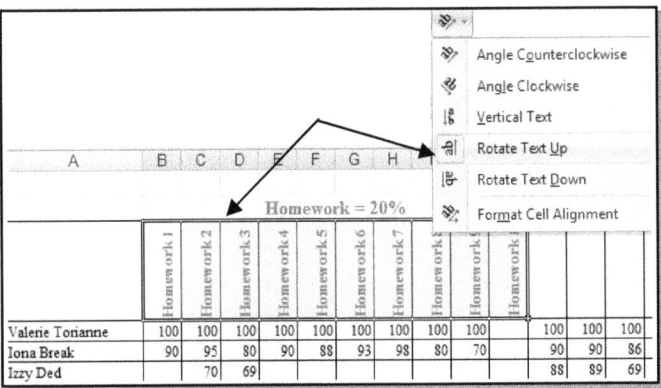

Wrapping text in a cell

When you type more text in a cell than the column width will allow, text will wrap to the next cell if it is empty. For long text entries, use the **Wrap Text** feature to wrap text to multiple lines. The height of the row will automatically increase. To wrap text in a cell:

♦ Highlight the cell(s).

♦ Click the [Wrap Text] button in the **Alignment** group on the **Home** tab.

- 43 -

Microsoft® Excel 2007   Quick Reference Guide

To center information across multiple cells

If you want to center a heading across the top of a report or center across multiple columns, use the merge and center icon on the **Home** tab.

	A	B	C	D	E
1		The Corner Gardens			
2		Plant Inventory			
3					
4			Tray Size		
5	Annual Flowers		8-6 packs	6-6 packs	Total Packs
6		Asters	25	25	350
7		Alyssum	30	25	390
8		Begonias	15	15	210
9		Cosmos	20	20	280
10		Dahlias	20	25	310
11		Dusty Miller	25	25	350
12		Gazanias	35	25	430
13		Impatiens	50	25	550
14		Marigolds	150	25	1,350
15		Pansies	125	25	1,150
16		Petunias	100	25	950
17		Salvia	10	10	140
18		Snapdragons	75	25	750
19		Statice	25	25	350
20		Greenhouse Total	705	320	7,560

(Merged Cells)

- Type the information in the first column that information will be centered across.
- Select the range of cells to center across.
- Click the **Merge and Center** icon on the **Home** tab.

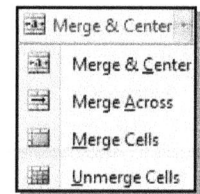

  - **Merge & Center** merges selected cells together and centers text. If multiple rows are highlighted, the rows will be merged together.
    This will keep the information in the upper left most cell only.

- 44 -

Microsoft® Excel 2007   Quick Reference Guide

- **Merge Across** merges selected cells but does not change the alignment. This is used when you want to select more than one row and merge cells across the rows.

- **Merge Cells** combines selected cells but does not change the alignment. If multiple rows are selected, Excel will only keep the data in the upper left most cells.

✎ To separate cells that have been merged, select the cells, click the drop-down arrow on the **Merge & Center** button on the **Home** tab. Click **Unmerge Cells**.

Using the alignment dialogue box

The Format Cell Alignment dialogue box includes all of the alignment choices in one area. To display alignment choices:

♦ Click the ▦ dialogue box launcher in the **Alignment** group on the **Home** tab.

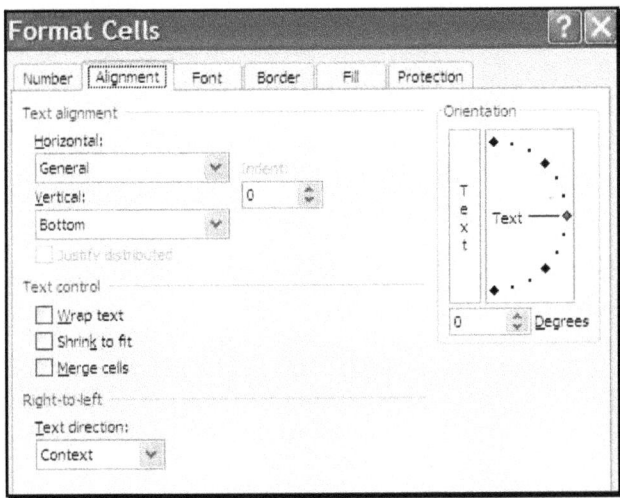

Choose from the following alignment choices:

Horizontal   Left-justify text, right-justify numbers,
General   and center all other logical and error
             values. This is the default, and the only

- 45 -

Microsoft® Excel 2007　　　Quick Reference Guide

	setting that treats text and numbers differently.
Horizontal Left (Indent) 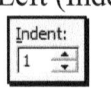	Aligns text on the left. Increase the Indent setting to indent text within a cell.
Horizontal Center	Centers text or numbers in a cell.
Horizontal Right (Indent)	Aligns text on the right. Increase the Indent setting to indent text on the right side of a cell.
Horizontal Fill	Fill selected cells by repeating the complete contents of each cell within the selection. For example, you can repeat the * to fill a cell with a series of **********
Horizontal Justify	Spreads wrapped lines across the cell width. The last line of the cell does not wrap.
Horizontal Center Across Selection	Used to center text across multiple cells.
Horizontal Distributed (Indent)	This allows you to distribute the contents evenly across the whole cell.
Vertical alignment	Set **Vertical** alignment to control whether text appears aligned at the top, bottom, center or justified. The appearance of text changes only when the height of the row is taller than the amount of text in the cell..
Wrapped text	**Wrap Text** is turned on, text that is

Microsoft® Excel 2007   Quick Reference Guide

	longer than the cell width wraps to new lines within the same cell.
Shrink to Fit	If you select Shrink to Fit, the font size in the cell will shrink if all text does not fit in the cell.
Merge Cells	Used to merge multiple cells together. Typically used to center a heading across multiple columns

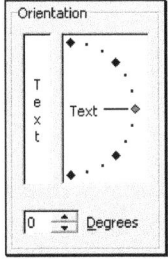
Set **Orientation** to determine the direction and orientation of text by dragging the red diamond on the orientation meter or by typing specific degrees for the text.

To copy formatting

When you copy the contents of a cell, the formatting is also copied. If you want to copy the format without copying the contents, use the format painter icon in the clipboard group on the **Home** tab.

♦ Select the cell that has the format you want to copy.

♦ Click the ▦ **Format Painter** icon in the **Clipboard** group of the **Home** tab.

♦ Select the cell(s) to receive the formatting.

⊕ If you double-click the Format Painter, it remains active until it is clicked again, allowing you to apply the formatting to multiple selections.

Microsoft® Excel 2007 Quick Reference Guide

Controlling Page Breaks & Column Titles

When you have a spreadsheet that is more than one page, you will find the following tools helpful in controlling column headings and page breaks.

Freeze titles in the spreadsheet window

When you scroll down in a spreadsheet the column headings disappear from the screen. To freeze the headings at the top or left side of the spreadsheet window:

- Click on the first cell below the titles. For example, if you want column A and rows 1-2 to stay on the screen when you scroll, click in B3.

- On the **View** tab, click the **Freeze Panes** button. A line will display between your data and titles. This line does not print.

In the above example, the user clicked in B7 and froze the headings in row 6 and Column A. As the user scrolls down or to the right, the headings do not disappear from the screen.

- To turn off the freeze pane feature, click the **Freeze Panes** button on the **View** tab and choose **Unfreeze Panes**.

✎ The Freeze Panes feature only controls titles in the spreadsheet window. To print column headings on every page, see page 36.

- 48 -

Microsoft® Excel 2007 — Quick Reference Guide

To insert manual page breaks

If your spreadsheet is more than one page, Excel automatically places the page breaks for you. Automatic page breaks appear in the worksheet after a file has been printed or previewed as short dashed lines. If you want to force page breaks on your own, use the manual page break feature.

- Select the cell that should begin the new page.

- On the **Page Layout** tab, click the **Breaks** button.

- Choose **Insert Page Break**.

- To remove a manual page break, position the cell pointer immediately below or to the right of the page break. On the **Page Layout** tab, click the **Breaks** button. Choose **Remove Page Break**.

Building Formulas

All formulas start with an =. They may contain cell addresses, numbers, arithmetic operators and Excel functions. Excel performs functions in the following order:

( )	^	*	/	+	-
Parentheses	Exponents	Multiplication	Division	Addition	Subtraction

To help remember the order of operation, think of this sentence:

Please	Excuse	My	Dear	Aunt	Sally

For example:

	A	B	C
1	5		2
2	3		
3			

=A1+A2*C1   equals 11
=(A1+A2)*C1   equals 16

To demonstrate how parentheses work using values, rather than cell addresses:

=2+2*3+3   equals 11
=(2+2)*3+3   equals 15
=2+2*(3+3)   equals 14
=(2+2)*(3+3)   equals 24

Excel does what is in parentheses first, then multiplication and then addition.

There are 2 basic ways to write a formula.

1) Type the cell reference for each cell that contains a value that will be calculated separated by an operator (+ - * /).
   Example:

   =A1+A2

2) Or use a special function. There are over 200 special function formulas built into Excel. Each one is a program in itself. The syntax for a special function is

   =FUNCTION(ARGUMENTS)

Microsoft® Excel 2007   Quick Reference Guide

Arguments are the pieces of information that Excel needs to perform the function. Each argument is separated by a comma. If an argument is a range of numbers, the range is separated by a colon.

For example:

=SUM(C5:C100)	Adds the range of numbers from C5 through C100
=SUM(C5,C100)	Adds only C5 and C100
=SUM(C5:C50,C100:C150)	Adds the range of C5 through C50 to the range of C100 through C150. In other words, it skips C51 through C99

To write a formula

- Click in the cell where the result of the formula will display. Type an =
- Type each individual cell address separated by an operator. For example type   =A1+A2
- Press [ENTER]. The result will display.

Or Type an = followed by a function name. Enclose the augments in parentheses.

Displaying help for special functions

To display a complete list of all functions:

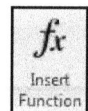

- Click the **Formulas** tab on the ribbon.
- Click the **Insert Function** button.
- Select a **Function Category** or choose **All**.

Microsoft® Excel 2007   Quick Reference Guide

- Highlight a function name and click **Help on this function** displayed in the lower left corner of the dialogue box. The help window will display after a short delay.

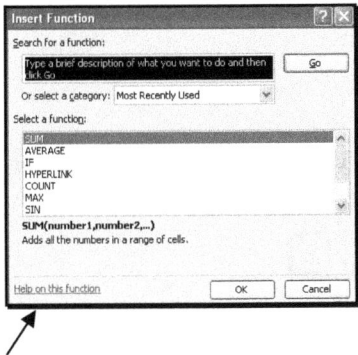

- Click the Insert Function button displayed at the beginning of the formula bar.

Using the AutoSum icon

The **Formulas** tab on the ribbon includes an **AutoSum** button to quickly add columns and rows.

- The AutoSum button has 2 parts. The top half of the button will quickly add the closest range of values. The bottom part of the button displays additional functions, i.e., Average, Min, Max or Count Numbers.

- A small AutoSum button also appears on the **Home** tab. The drop-down arrow can be used to perform other common functions including Average, Count, Max, Min or click More Functions to display a complete list.

To add a column or row of numbers

- Move the cell pointer to a blank cell below the column of numbers or at the end of a row.

- Click the AutoSum icon, change the range if necessary and press [ENTER].

Microsoft® Excel 2007   Quick Reference Guide

To create totals below several columns

- Select a range of empty cells at the bottom of the columns you want to total.
- Click the AutoSum button.

To create grand totals

- Select all of the subtotals as well as the cells they add, and include a blank cell for the grand totals.
- Click the AutoSum button [Σ].

Absolute Referencing (also known as Absolute Addressing)

When a formula is copied to another cell, cell references in the formula change relative to the new cell location. If a formula is copied down, the row number will increase in each row. If a formula is copied across, the column letter will increase in each column. This is known as *relative addressing* because the formula becomes relative to the new address.

In the example below, the cell reference to C3 is relative and increases the row number each time it is copied down. The cell reference to G1 is an absolute and remains the same when the formula is copied.

B	C	D	E	F	G
				Mileage Rate	0.48
Destination and Return	R/T Mileage	Mileage Allowance			
Concord	52	=C3*$G$1			
Manchester	88	=C4*$G$1			
Portsmouth	102	=C5*$G$1			
Exeter	98	=C6*$G$1			
Laconia	12	=C7*$G$1			

Microsoft® Excel 2007　　　　Quick Reference Guide

Example: Relative Referencing

Original formula in cell B16:　　=SUM(B9:B15)
Copied across to cell C16:　　=SUM(C9:C15)

Original formula in cell F8:　　=SUM(B8:E8)
Copied down to cell F9:　　=SUM(B9:E9)

	A	B	C	D	E	F
5	Department:				Rate/Mile:	0.44
6						
7		Monday	Tuesday	Wednesday	Thursday	Wkly Totals
8	# Miles	130	96	98	0	=SUM(B8:E8)
9	Mileage Amount	=B8*$F$5	=C8*$F$5	=D8*$F$5	=E8*$F$5	=SUM(B9:E9)
10	Air Transportation	0	0	211.5	0	=SUM(B10:E10)
11	Hotel/Lodging	0	0	93.52	93.52	=SUM(B11:E11)
12	Meals	0	0	20	62	=SUM(B12:E12)
13	Office Supplies	139.95	41	0	0	=SUM(B13:E13)
14	Parking & Tolls	3.75	2.5	20	20	=SUM(B14:E14)
15						
16	Total	=SUM(B9:B15)	=SUM(C9:C15)	=SUM(D9:D15)	=SUM(E9:E15)	=SUM(F9:F15)

When formulas include cell references that should not change during a copy, they are called *absolute references*. An absolute reference has a $ in front of the column letter and in front of the row number. Absolute references do not change when they are copied to another location.

Example: Absolute Referencing

Original formula in cell B9:　　= B8*$F$5
Copied across to cell C9:　　= C8*$F$5

To write a formula with an absolute reference

♦ Type the $ as part of the cell reference.

Or press [F4] after typing or pointing to the cell reference.

Microsoft® Excel 2007 — Quick Reference Guide

Using Paste Function

There are over 200 special functions formulas built into Excel. They can be used individually or as part of larger formulas. The syntax for using a special function is

=FUNCTION(ARGUMENTS)

Arguments are the pieces of information that are needed to execute the specified function. Arguments are separated by a comma. If an argument is a range, the range is separated by a colon. Do not type any spaces within a function. Example

=SUM(C1:C10)	This formula has one argument. It adds the range of values from C1 to C10.
=SUM(C1,C10,C25,C50)	This has 4 arguments. It adds the values in the individual cells.
=SUM(C1:C10,C25:C50)	This formula has 2 arguments. It adds the range of C1 through C10 to the range of C25 through C50.

Sample Special Function Formulas

=SUM(C1:C10)	Add the range of values from C1 to C10.
=AVERAGE(C1:C10)	Displays the average of all numbers from C1 to C10.
=MIN(C1:C10)	Display the smallest value in the range C1 through C10.
=MAX(C1:C10)	Display the largest value in the range C1 through C10.

Microsoft® Excel 2007   Quick Reference Guide

=COUNT(C1:C10)   Counts all values within the specified range.

=COUNTA(C1:C10)   Counts all non-blank cells within the specified range.

=COUNTBLANK(C1:C10)   Counts all blank cells within the specified range.

=PMT(C7/12,C8,-C6)   Calculates a loan payment based on:

C7 is the interest rate divided by 12

C8 is the term (number of payments)

C6 is the amount borrowed (this should be negative)

To use Paste Function

- Position the cell pointer where you want the formula. Click the Paste Function button.

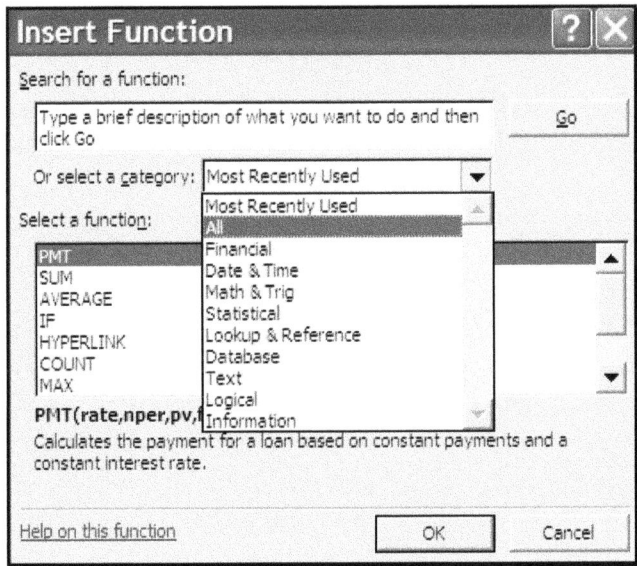

- Select a **Function Category** and a **Function Name**. The selected function's description and format appear at the bottom of the dialog box. Click OK.
- Provide a value, cell reference, or range name for each argument. Required arguments appear in bold; optional arguments may be omitted. The value of each argument appears to the right, and the calculated **Value** of the function appears at the bottom of the dialogue box.
- Click OK when all arguments have been defined.
- If you need examples or additional information on a special function, click `Help on this function` in the lower left corner of the Paste Function dialogue box.

Microsoft® Excel 2007   Quick Reference Guide

PMT

The PMT formula calculates a monthly loan payment. The result is always negative because it represents a cost. If you want the result to display as a positive number precede the principal amount with a negative sign [-]

Format: PMT(rate,nper,pv)

Arguments: Rate - interest rate, usually divided by 12 to convert annual to monthly

Nper – is the number of periods or otherwise known as the term of the loan in months.

Pv – present value or the loan amount.

Examples: =PMT(11.25%/12,48,10000)   ($259.67)

=PMT(.0975/12,360,120000)   ($1,030.99)

=PMT(.0975/12,360,–120000) $1,030.99

=ROUND(PMT(Interest/12,Term,Principal) ,2)   Rounds payment to 2 decimals

Microsoft® Excel 2007   Quick Reference Guide

ROUND

This formula rounds a value to the specified number of decimal places. The rounded result is used in further calculations.

Format: ROUND(number,num_digits)

Arguments: Number - the constant, cell reference, or formula to be rounded.

num_digits - the number of decimal places to round the number to, which can be positive, negative, or zero.

	A	B
1	Cost Per Gallon	Selling Price
2	1.642	

To calculate the selling price using round:

Examples: =ROUND(A2,3)   1.642
              =ROUND(A2,2)   1.64
              =ROUND(A2,1)   1.60
              =ROUND(A2,0)   2.00

Variations of Round

Examples: =ROUNDUP(A2,2)   1.65
              =ROUNDDOWN(A2,1)   1.60

Microsoft® Excel 2007   Quick Reference Guide

IF

Purpose   tests a condition, and displays one result if the condition is true, another if the condition is false.

Format: IF(TEST,TRUE,FALSE)

Arguments: logical TEST: compares two values or expressions separated by one of the following:

    =   equal to
    <   less than
    >   greater than
    <=   less than or equal to
    >=   greater than or equal to
    <>   not equal to

TRUE: result if the test is true. This argument is optional. If it is omitted, a true test displays the result TRUE.

FALSE: result if the test is false. This argument is optional. If it is omitted, a false test displays the result FALSE.

✎ If the result should display text, enclose text in quotes.

Examples: =IF(A3>10,A5,B5)
              =IF(RATE*B4>=16,RATE*10,0)
              =A3*(IF(D1>15,D1,1)
              =IF(D11<E11,"YES","NO")

Microsoft® Excel 2007   Quick Reference Guide

IF Statement Examples

	A	B	C	D	E	F	G	H
4								
5								
6	TO:	Customer Name			Number:	1010		
7		Street Address						
8		City, State Zip			Date:	09/09/08		
9								
10		ATTN: Contact Person						
11								
12								
13								
14								
15	Date	Description of Services			Hours	Rate/hr	Amt Due	
16								
17	8/30/08	Intro to Computers Class			3.00	37.50	=IF(D17<1,E17,D17*E17)	
18	9/6/08	Consulting/Troubleshooting			0.75	37.50	37.50	
19								

	A	B	C	D	E	F	G	H
1		Residential Mortgage - Non-Performing Loans						
2		90 Days+						
3		September 2008						
4								
5								
6	Borrower	Principal Balance	Negative Escrow	Unpaid Taxes	75% Property Appraisal	Estimated Loss		
7								
8	Willie Makit	$84,854.37	$2,889.86	$0.00	$56,775.00	=IF(SUM(B8:D8)<E8,0,B8-E8+C8+D8)		
9	Ena Dett	$51,066.78	$1,371.02	$0.00	$30,000.00	$22,437.80		
10	Y. R. Ulate	$87,657.44	$628.18	$0.00	$63,750.00	$24,535.62		
11	Kent Payette	$69,907.37	$1,681.20	$0.00	$93,525.00	$0.00		
12	Justin F. Gott	$55,988.59	$3,281.55	$0.00	$42,000.00	$17,270.14		
13	Izzy Ded	$69,861.42	$750.01	$0.00	$61,650.00	$8,961.43		
14	Ben Restin	$35,319.14	$5,522.55	$0.00	$75,450.00	$0.00		

Microsoft® Excel 2007   Quick Reference Guide

Lookup Functions

VLOOKUP and HLOOKUP

Purpose: The lookup functions VLOOKUP and HLOOKUP are used to find a value in a table or an array. The table must consist of one or more rows and columns. The leftmost column contains the lookup values, which must be in ascending order if they are numbers.

Format: VLOOKUP(LookupValue,Table,Col#, RangeLookup)

HLOOKUP(LookupValue,Table,Row#,RangeLookup)

Arguments: **LookupValue**: used to determine which row (or column) of the table to use. If the LookupValue is a number, Excel uses the last row (or column) in the table whose 1st value is less than or equal to the LookupValue. If the LookupValue is a label, Excel uses the 1st row (or column) of the table that matches. Note: If the LookupValue is a number, the numbers must be in ascending order.

Table: location of the array of values, may be a defined name.

Column#: specifies the column (row) of the table the result should be taken from. 1 indicates that the result comes from the 1st column (row), 2 from the 2nd, etc.

RangeLookup: is an *optional* argument. If you specify this argument to be TRUE or omit the argument, Excel will find the closest match. If you specify this argument as FALSE, Excel looks for an exact match. If one is not found, the error value #N/A is returned.

Microsoft® Excel 2007 — Quick Reference Guide

Examples: In the following example the VLOOKUP formula locates the Vacation Days Earned by locating the Years of Employment in the first column of the Table Range and returns the value listed in Column #2 of the table.

	A	B	C	D	E	F
1	*The Corner Gardens*				Table Range	
2	*Vacation Schedule*					
3	LookUp Value					
4	Employee Name	Years of Employment	Vacation Days Earned		Yrs of Employment	Days Earned
5	Mary Gold	18	=VLOOKUP(B5,table,2)		0	0
6	Mark E. Ting	12			1	5
7	Rose Busch	9			5	10
8	Holly Hawk	1			10	15
9	Daisy Fields	4			15	20
10	Lilly Day	3			20	25

Working With Text in a Formula

If a formula includes text, it must be enclosed in parentheses. Otherwise Excel assumes the text refers to a range name. If you want to join two text fields together in a formula use the & symbol. The sample below joins the text in A2 and the text in B2 to display the full name in column C. Because we want a space between the first and last name, the space must be enclosed in quotes.

	A	B	C
1	**FIRST**	**LAST**	**NAME**
2	Rose	Busch	=A2&" "&B2
3	Daisy	Fields	Daisy Fields
4	Luke	Umber	Luke Umber
5	Daphne	Dill	Daphne Dill
6	Lou	Pinn	Lou Pinn
7	Brock	Lee	Brock Lee
8	Mary	Gold	Mary Gold
9	Tom A.	Toe	Tom A. Toe

Microsoft® Excel 2007   Quick Reference Guide

Defining and Using Range Names

In Excel, formulas, values, cells, and groups of cells can be given names like PRICE, DISCOUNT, and TOTALS. Names must be unique, can be up to 255 characters long, and may include only letters, numbers and the characters _ . ? \ Names are created as absolute references, and are not adjusted during copy or clipboard operations.

When selected cells have been named, the name appears in the names box at the beginning of the formula bar. Names can be substituted in commands, formulas, and functions whenever the cells they refer to would be used.

To define a name

- Select the cell(s) you want to name, click in the Name Box on the formula bar, type the new name, and press [ENTER].
- or Select the cell(s) you want to name. Click the **Formulas** tab and click **Define Name**. Type a name for the cell(s) and click OK.

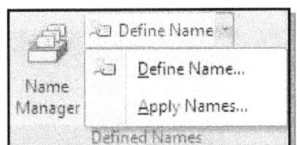

✎ If Excel finds an appropriate text constant in the cell to the left of or above the selected area, it suggests the text as a name. Accept or change the name.

If you define a name that already exists, the new definition replaces the old. As each name is highlighted, its cell address appears in the **Refers to** box

To select and go to a named cell or range

- Press [CTRL][G] and double-click the name.
- or Click the Name Box drop down list at the beginning of the formula bar and click a name.

- 65 -

To automatically create names from data

If you have an existing list that you want to use to create names for adjacent cells, use the Create from Selection feature.

- Select the area that includes the labels and the cells you want to assign names to.
- Click the **Formulas** tab.
- Click the [Create from Selection] button.
- Select the appropriate check box and click OK.
- In this example, Excel will use the labels in the left column to names the cells in the right column. For example, 130 will be named Bennington, 52 will be named Concord, etc.

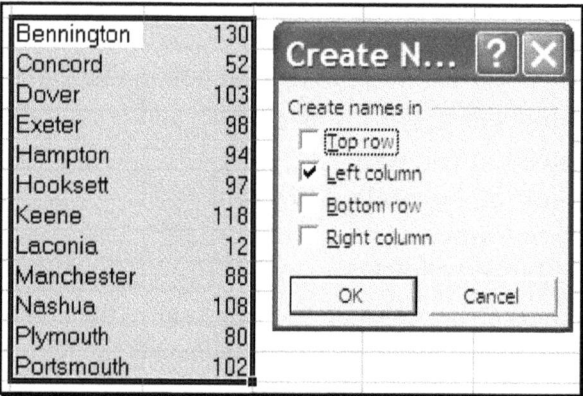

✎ You can write a formula =**Concord*.48** and Excel will use the 52 that has been named Concord and multiply the value times .48

Create a reference list of existing range names

If you have many range names in a workbook, you may want to create a list of the names and the cells they refer to.

- Click on an empty area of the workbook.
- Click the **Formulas** tab. Click the **Use in Formula** button and choose **Paste Names**.

Microsoft® Excel 2007   Quick Reference Guide

- Click the **Paste List** button. This writes a list of names and references into the sheet starting at the active cell location. The list is written in 2 columns, down from the active cell, and to the right of it, so be sure this area is empty before you executive this function.

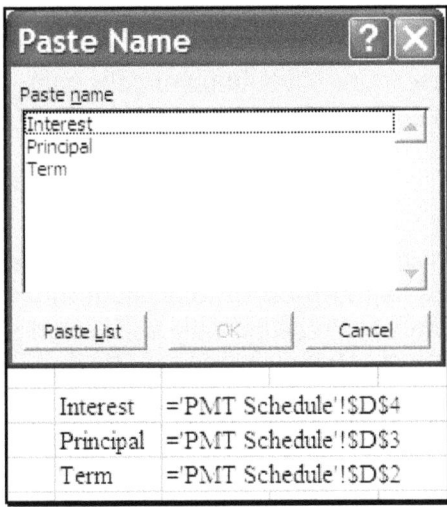

To delete a name

- On the **Formulas** tab, click the **Name Manager** button.
- Highlight the name and click the **Delete** button.

To insert a name into a formula

- Create a formula and type the name into the formula.

Or Use the point and click method to write the formula.

   Type an =

   Click the first cell to be used in the calculation

   Type an operator -- + - * /

   Click the next cell to be used in the formula

   Press enter to complete writing the formula.

- 67 -

Microsoft® Excel 2007   Quick Reference Guide

Term (months)	36
Principal Amount	30,000.00
Interest Rate	11%
Monthly Payment	=PMT(Interest/12,Term,-Principal)

✎ The intersection of 2 defined names may be used as a cell reference. The intersection of a column of cells named *Feb* with a row named *Wages* can be referred to as *=Feb Wages*.

Using Auditing Tools

Audit tools are used to add arrow pointers to a worksheet to show the cells that have been included in a formula or to locate formulas that are dependent on other formulas. *Precedents* are cells referred to in formulas within the selected cell. *Dependents* are cells containing formulas that refer to the selected cell. The arrows added to a sheet when using Trace Precedents or Trace Dependents are automatically removed when you close the file.

To Trace Precedents

- Position the cell pointer on a formula.
- Click the **Formulas** tab. Click the **Trace Precedents** button. Arrows will display to show the values included in the formula.

To Trace Dependents

- Position the cell pointer on a value or select a range of values.
- Click the **Formulas** tab. Click the **Trace Dependents** button. Arrows will display to show formulas that include the selected cells.

Microsoft® Excel 2007　　　　　　　Quick Reference Guide

Greenhouse Construction	Price Each	Projected Amount
5 40 x 100 Greenhouse Frame	950.00	4,750.00
5 Rolls 3-year plastic	299.00	1,495.00
75 Tables for plants	30.00	2,250.00
5 Furnace heating system for each house	1,250.00	6,250.00
10 Large Exhaust fan/cooling system	325.00	3,250.00
5 Pipe for watering system fertization	850.00	4,250.00
Total Greenhouse Construction		$22,245.00

To remove trace arrows

Click the **Formulas** tab. Click the **Remove Arrows** button.

Working with Multiple Sheets

When a *workbook* is first created in Excel, it contains 3 sheets. A workbook can have a maximum of 255 sheets. Each sheet may contain a worksheet, chart, macro sheet, etc. Sheets may be inserted, deleted, copied, and moved within the current workbook or between other workbooks.

The default number of sheets in a new file can be changed by clicking the Office button and choosing **Excel Options.** To set your preference, click the **Popular** tab and change

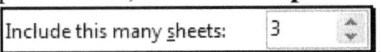
.

Sheet tabs display at the left end of the horizontal scroll bar.

To display a sheet

- Click the sheet tab name at the bottom of the screen.

To rename a sheet

- Double-click the sheet tab, type a new name and press [ENTER]. Sheet tab names can be typed in upper or lowercase and may contain spaces or numbers. The size of the tab will adjust to the number of characters you type.

Grouping sheets

When sheets are grouped, any information that is typed, deleted, moved, copied or formatted will apply to all sheets in the group.

To group

- All sheets - *right-click* on any sheet tab and choose **Select All Sheets**.
- Random sheets - hold the [CTRL] key and click the sheet tabs to be grouped.

- A range of sheets - select the first sheet by clicking the sheet tab, hold the [SHIFT] key and click the last sheet to be grouped.

To ungroup

- All sheets - *Right-click* on a selected sheet tab and choose **Ungroup All Sheets**.
- Individual sheets - hold the [CTRL] key and click the sheets to be ungrouped.

✎ If you click a sheet tab that is not in the group, all sheet tabs will be ungrouped automatically.

To copy or move a sheet within the same workbook

- To change the order of sheets in a workbook, point to the sheet tab and drag it to a new location.
- To copy a sheet within a workbook, point to the sheet tab, hold the [CTRL] key and drag the tab to the new location. Release the mouse *before* releasing the [CTRL] key. The new sheet name will display with (2) at the end of the current name. Double-click to rename the sheet.

To copy a sheet to a new workbook

- Open both the source and target workbook.
- From the *source* file that contains the sheet to be copied, *right-click* on the sheet tab.
- Choose **Move or Copy**.
- Choose the *target* workbook from the **To Book** drop-down menu.
- Specify the new location for the sheet from the **Before Sheet** listing.
- Select **Create a Copy** if the sheet should remain in both the source and target files.

✎ To switch between open workbooks press [CTRL][F6]. The original source file may be closed after copying.

Microsoft® Excel 2007   Quick Reference Guide

To insert a sheet between existing sheets

- *Right-click* the sheet tab and choose **Insert, Worksheet**.

  Or Click the **Insert Worksheet** tab

To permanently delete a sheet

- ***SAVE FIRST***. Deleted Sheets can not be brought back with undo.
- *Right-click* the sheet tab and choose **Delete**.

Change the color of a sheet tab

- *Right-click* the sheet tab and choose **Tab Color**.
- Choose a color, click OK.

View multiple sheets in a workbook

- For each sheet tab that should have a separate window, click the **New Window** button on the View tab of the ribbon.
- Click **Arrange All**. Specify how you want to arrange windows on the screen.

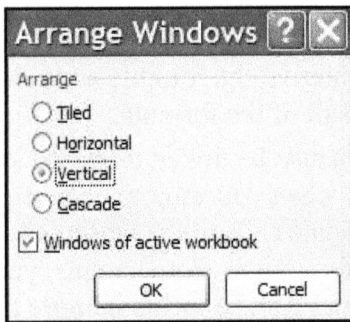

➥ To close each window, click the close box at the end of each title bar. Click the Maximize button at the end of the title bar to enlarge the workbook to fill the Excel window.

- 73 -

Microsoft® Excel 2007   Quick Reference Guide

Linking formulas between sheets

Formulas in a workbook can be written across sheets to perform calculations. The syntax for formulas is:
=Sheetname!cell+Sheetname!cell.

For example,

Plant Production, First Year			
=Supplies!G52/100	Plant Trays (Box of 100)	29.00	413.85
=Supplies!F52/100	Plant Markers (Box of 100)	0.79	90.19
	Cost of seeds (see attached supplies sheet)		=Supplies!E52

- Formulas can be built by using the point and click method.
  - Position the cell pointer where you want the result to display.
  - Type an = to begin writing the formula.
  - Switch to the sheet that contains the first value to be calculated and click the cell. The sheetname and cell address displays on the formula bar.
  - Type an operator, + - * or /.
  - Click the next cell to be calculated, switching sheets if necessary.
  - Continue clicking cells to be calculated separated by an operator.
  - Press [ENTER] to complete entering the formula and return to the cell that contains the result of the formula.
- Cells with text or values can also be linked using the steps show above. This is useful when you want to change information in a cell and update cells in the workbook that should display the same information. For example, you may have a form where a customer name appears in more than one location. If you change the source cell, the target cell that contains a link will also update.

Microsoft® Excel 2007 Quick Reference Guide

Worksheet Links

Excel workbooks may contain formulas that include *external references* to cells or names in other workbooks. The workbook that contains the formula that refers to another workbook is called the *dependent workbook*. A workbook that is referenced in another workbook's formulas is called a *source workbook*.

Format: An external reference includes the name of the workbook (enclosed in square brackets [ ]), the sheet (followed by an exclamation point !), and the cell reference. If the source workbook has a different path from the dependent workbook, the path must precede the filename, and the path, filename, and sheet name must be enclosed in single quotes ' '. The cell reference may be a single cell, a range, or a defined name.

Examples:

=[BUDGET]January!A7
=SUM('C:\DATAFILES\[SALES]Sheet1'!$A$45:$K$115
='E:\FILES\[EXPENSES.XLS]DIV6'!TOTALS

To create a link

- Type the entire external reference as part of the formula.
- or Be sure the source workbook is open. Create the formula by pointing instead of typing. When the external reference is needed, switch to the source workbook and select the cell(s) needed. Excel creates the external reference for you.

  Changes to source workbooks are automatically reflected in active dependent workbooks. While a source workbook is open, its external reference displays without a path. When a source workbook is not open, its external references display with the path.

Microsoft® Excel 2007   Quick Reference Guide

✎ To remove an external reference, delete the formula or use **Copy** and **Paste Special** to convert the external reference to a value.

To update links to unopened books

- Choose **Yes** (if prompted) to update the links when you open a dependent workbook.
- or At any time, choose **Edit Links**, on the Data tab of the ribbon. Select one or more **Source File** names, and choose **Update Values**.

Charts & Drawing Objects

Creating a Chart

- Select the range of data to be plotted, including column and row labels. The range may include several nonadjacent areas, as long as Excel can logically combine them into a single rectangle to plot.
- Click the **Insert** tab on the ribbon.
- Click a chart type button in the Charts group.

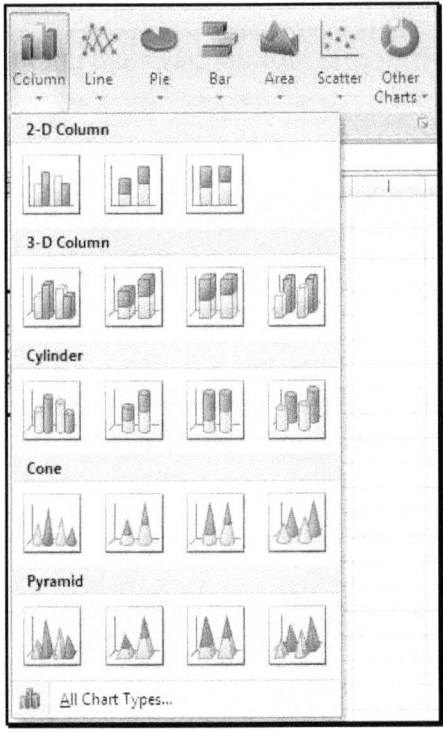

- Click the chart subtype. Excel automatically creates an embedded chart on the same sheet as the data and new Chart tabs appear on the ribbon.

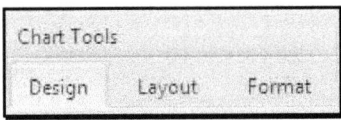

✎ An *embedded chart* is embedded on a sheet. If a chart will be printed on the same page with other charts, or with spreadsheet data, it must be an embedded chart.

A *Chart Sheet* places the chart on its own sheet in the workbook and is sized to fit the entire page.

To change an embedded chart to a chart sheet

* Click in the chart area to select the embedded chart.
* On the **Design** tab in the Chart Tools group, click the **Move Chart Location** button.
* Click **New Sheet**, type a name for the sheet and click OK.

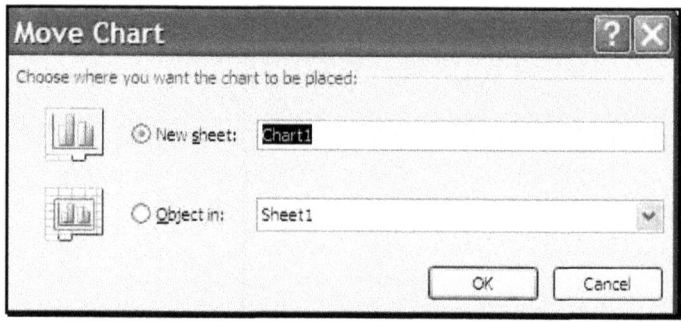

Microsoft® Excel 2007   Quick Reference Guide

Chart components

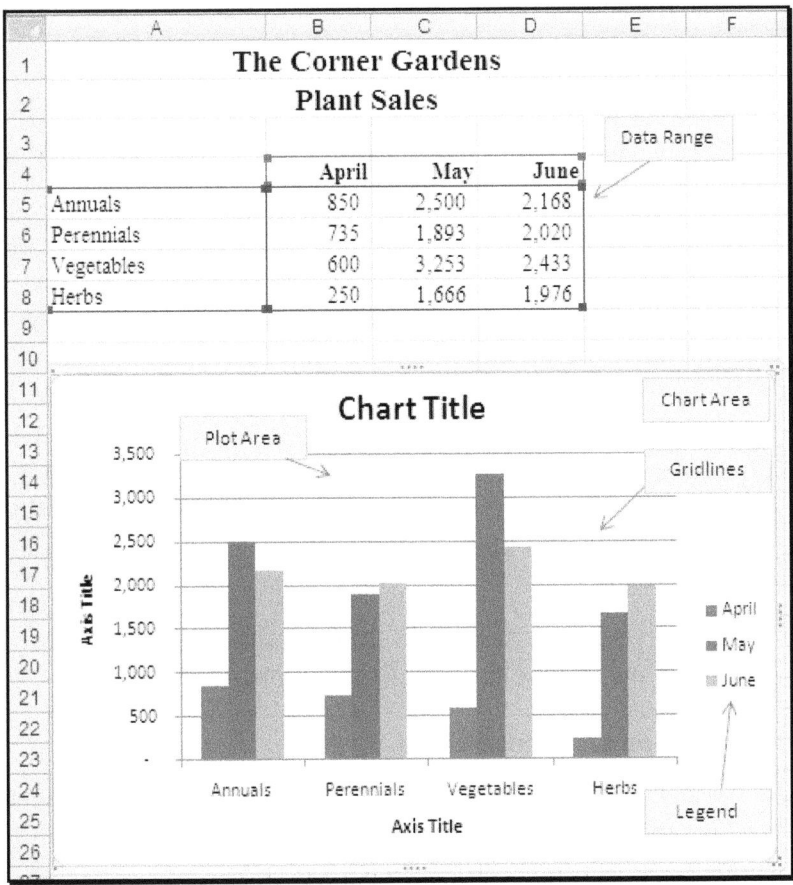

Chart area	contains the plot area legend, titles, category names, and axis values.
Plot area	contains the plotted data, usually a rectangle bounded at the bottom by the X-axis and on the left by the Y-axis.
X-axis	usually horizontal, plots time periods, regions, or groups.

Microsoft® Excel 2007   Quick Reference Guide

Y-axis	usually vertical, plots quantities, such as $s, units, hours, scores, temperatures, or volumes.
Category names	are names that appear along the X-axis.
Series names	are usually names that appear in the *legend*.
Data series	is the data values represented by one name that appears in the legend. Each data series has one value for each category.

Activating a chart

To customize chart options, the chart area must be activated. When a chart is activated the Chart Tools group appears on the ribbon and includes the Design, Layout and Format tabs. When you click outside the chart area to deselect the chart, these tabs disappear.

- To activate a chart, click in the chart area. A selection border and sizing handles display around the chart.

To resize an embedded chart

- Select the chart by clicking in the chart area. A thin selection box appears around the chart.
- Position the mouse pointer on a corner handles. The mouse pointer will change to a ↔ two headed arrow. Drag to change its size.

To move an embedded chart

- Position the mouse pointer in the chart area. The mouse pointer will be a four-headed arrow. Drag to move the chart.

Microsoft® Excel 2007   Quick Reference Guide

Editing Charts

When values in the original data sheet are changed, the chart will update automatically. If you insert a column or row within the original data range, the chart will update to include the new column/row.

If new columns or rows of data are inserted outside the original data range that was charted, the information must be copied to the chart.

Switch plotted data range from Column to Row

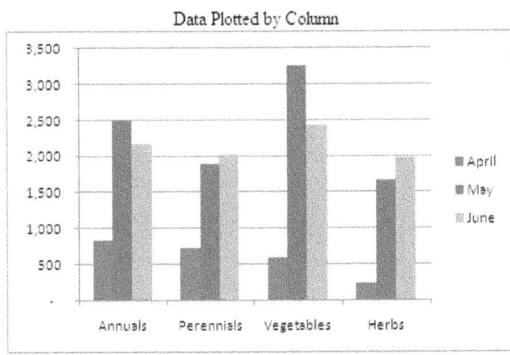

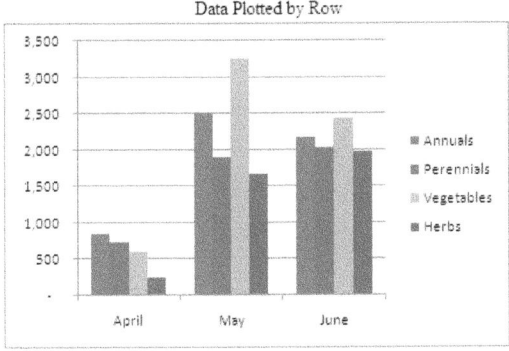

- Click in the chart area to select.
- Click the **Design** tab.
- Click **Switch Row/Column**.

Microsoft® Excel 2007   Quick Reference Guide

To copy new data to an embedded chart

- Select the data to be copied.
- Click the [Copy] Copy tool.
- Click in the chart area to select the chart and click [Paste].

Or Click the chart area. A border will display around the data range. Point to the corner of the data range – the mouse pointer will change to a 2 headed arrow. Click and drag to change the data range.

	A	B	C	D
1		The Corner Gardens		
2		Plant Sales		
3				
4		April	May	June
5	Annuals	850	2,500	2,168
6	Perennials	735	1,893	2,020
7	Vegetables	600	3,253	2,433
8	Herbs	250	1,666	1,976
9	Trees	900	3,800	2,500
10				

To copy new data to a chart sheet

- Select the data to be copied and click the copy icon on the Standard toolbar.
- Switch to the chart sheet and click Paste.

To chart multiple ranges

Most charts are created by selecting a range of cells that are adjacent. Occasionally, you may want to chart separate ranges that are not connected. For example, choose labels from Column A, and totals from Column D. To chart nonadjacent ranges

- Select the first range.
- Hold the [CTRL] key and select additional ranges.

Microsoft® Excel 2007   **Quick Reference Guide**

- Click the Insert on the ribbon and create the chart using the steps described on page 77.

	A	B	C	D	E
1		The Corner Gardens			
2		Plant Sales			
3					
4		April	May	June	Total
5	Annuals Flowers	850	2,500	2,168	5,518
6	Perennials	735	1,893	2,020	4,648
7	Vegetables	600	3,253	2,433	6,286
8	Herbs	250	1,666	1,976	3,892

- The steps above can also be used to edit the range of an existing chart.
  - Click in the chart area to select it.
  - Click the **Design** tab on the ribbon.
  - Click the **Select Data** button.
  - Click and drag to select the first data range.
  - Hold [CTRL] and select each additional range. Click OK.

Microsoft® Excel 2007   Quick Reference Guide

Changing the Chart Type

- Select the entire chart or a data series.
- Click the **Design** tab on the ribbon.
- Click the **Change Chart Type** button.

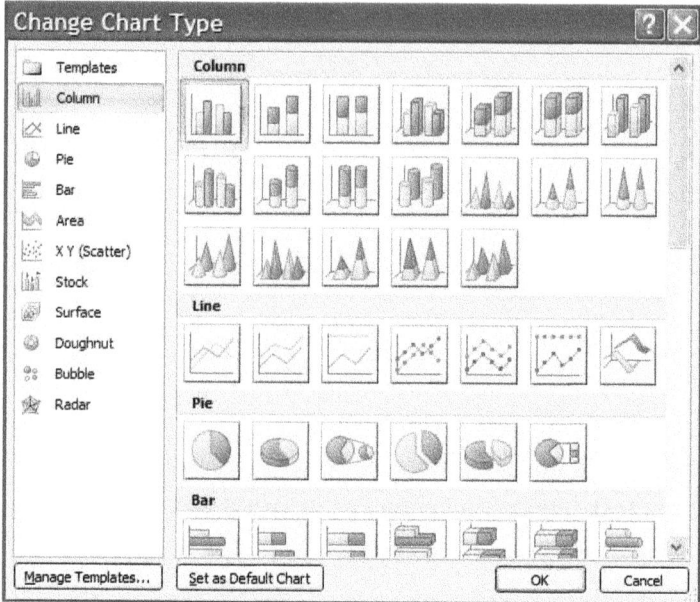

- Click the chart type and click OK.

Microsoft® Excel 2007   Quick Reference Guide

Customizing a Chart

All parts of a chart can be customized. There are several methods to use when you want to customize:

- ♦ Choose from pre-defined chart styles and layouts.
- Or Right-click the part of the chart you want to customize and choose from the shortcut menu.

To change the chart style

Excel offers many predefined chart formats that can be applied to a chart. The custom chart types set the background color, format for the title and data labels, legend, fonts and other chart format options.

- ♦ Activate the chart by clicking in the chart area
- ♦ Click the **Design** tab on the ribbon.

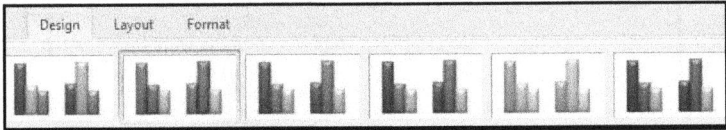

- ♦ Choose a **Chart Style**.

Choosing from pre-defined Chart Layouts

Chart Layouts quickly format charts to include titles, attach the data table, change the position of the legend, remove the scale & gridlines add values to a data series and many more. To choose a layout to customize the appearance of a chart:

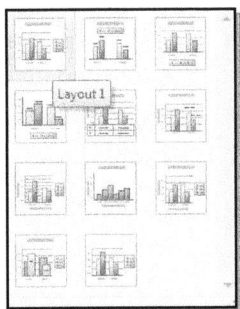

- ♦ Click the **Design** tab on the ribbon.
- ♦ Click one of the Chart Layouts.

- 85 -

Microsoft® Excel 2007 Quick Reference Guide

Customizing Chart Layout

Chart Layout options control the appearance of titles, the legend, data labels, the data table and gridlines. In addition, you can format the plot area, chart area and control 3D effects.

To add chart and axis titles

- To add or remove titles, select the chart and click the **Layout** tab.
- Click the **Chart Title** button and choose the location for the title. This creates a text box on the chart. Click the box and type your text.
- Click the **Axis Titles** button. Highlight **Primary Horizontal Axis Title** or **Primary Vertical Axis Titles** and click the appropriate Title setting. Type the title text.

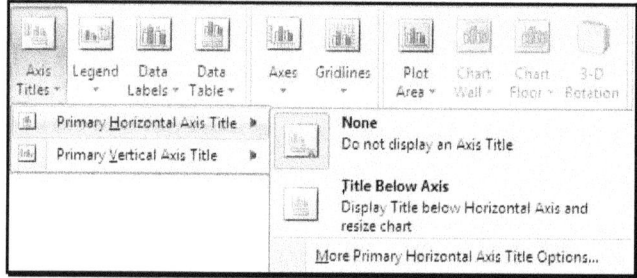

- To format a title, *right-click* the title and choose **Format Chart Title**. Use **Fill**, **Border Color** and **Style**, **Shadow**, 3D and **Alignment** to control the appearance of the title.

To customize the chart axes

- Click the chart area to select.
- Click the **Layout** tab on the ribbon
- Click the **Axes** button.
- Highlight **Primary Horizontal Axis** or **Primary Vertical Axis**.

Microsoft® Excel 2007   Quick Reference Guide

- Click one of the preset options or click **More Primary Horizontal Axis Options** or **More Primary Horizontal Axis Options**.

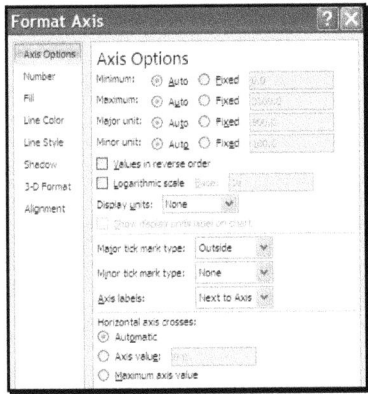

To customize the chart legend

- Click the chart area to select.
- Click the **Layout** tab on the ribbon
- Click the **Legend** button and choose the legend location or click **More Legend Options**.
- Right-click the legend and choose **Format Legend** to display legend formatting options.

To customize the data markers for a series

- Right-click a series and choose **Format Data Series**.
- **Series Options** offers choices to adjust the gap width, overlap a series or plot series or Primary or Secondary Axis. Note: These options change depending on the chart type.
- **Fill** controls the appearance of the data series. For example you can add a shaded

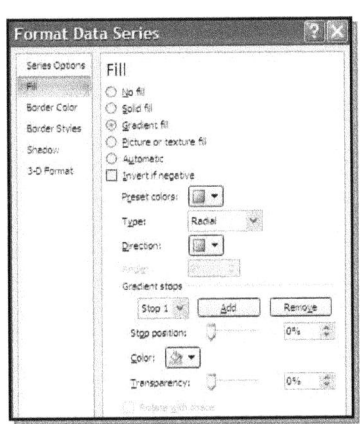

effect using the Gradient fill.

- **Border Color**, **Border Style**, **Shadow** and **3-D Format** provide additional formatting options to control the appearance of the series.

To customize an individual data marker (Data Point)

- Click to select the data series.
- Click a second time to isolate a data point.
- Right-click and choose **Format Data Point**. The settings you change are applied to the selected data point only.

To use a picture in data markers

- Right-click the data marker to receive the picture.
- Choose **Format Data Series**. Click **Fill** in the list on the left side of the dialogue box.
- Click **Insert from: File...**
- Locate the image you want to use and double-click the filename.

Stretch stretches one copy of the picture to fill the data marker.

Stack stacks multiple copies of the picture, in the picture's original proportions, to fill the data marker.

Stack and Scale With xx Units/Picture allows you to set the units to match the scale in your chart.

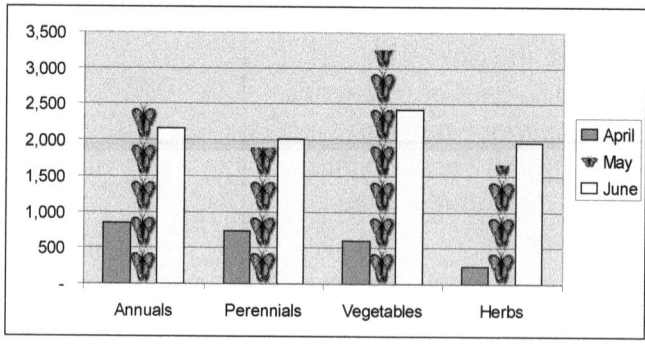

Customizing the Scale

You can customize the scale by changing the number format, adjusting the scale unit, minimum, maximum or remove the scale completely.

To remove the scale

- Right-click on any number in the scale.
- Choose **Delete**.

To turn the scale back on

- Select the chart.
- Click the **Layout** tab.
- Click the **Axes** button. Highlight Primary Vertical Axis and choose **Show Default Axis**.

To format the scale

- Right-click on any number in the scale.
- Click **Format Axis**
- Click a format category on the left and set your preferences. For example, use Number to change the number format.

To add values to data markers

- Right-click on a data marker.
- Click **Add Data Labels**.
- To format the data labels, right-click on the values and choose **Format Data Labels**.
- Use the **Alignment** option to rotate the values 90 degrees.
- Choose **Label Options** to change the position of the label. For example, center the label on the bar.

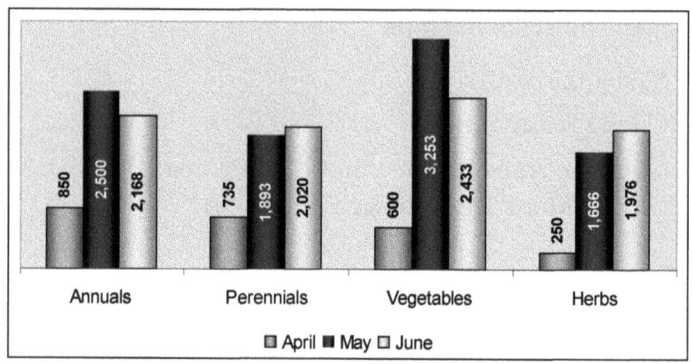

To customize the gridlines

- Right-click a gridline.
- Choose **Format Gridlines**.
- Set the **Line Color**, **Style** and **Shadow** options.

To remove Gridlines

- Click to select the chart. On the **Layout** tab, click the **Gridlines** button, highlight **Primary Horizontal Gridlines** and choose **None**.

Or Right-click on a gridline and choose **Delete**.

To customize the plot area

- Select the plot area and drag an edge or corner to move or resize it.

Microsoft® Excel 2007   Quick Reference Guide

- Right-click anywhere in the plot area that is not a specific chart element, and click **Format Plot Area**.

To customize the chart area

- Right-click anywhere in the chart that is not a specific chart element and choose **Format Chart Area**.
- To change the appearance use **Fill**, **Border color**, **Border Style**, **Shadow** and **3-D format**.

Chart Area
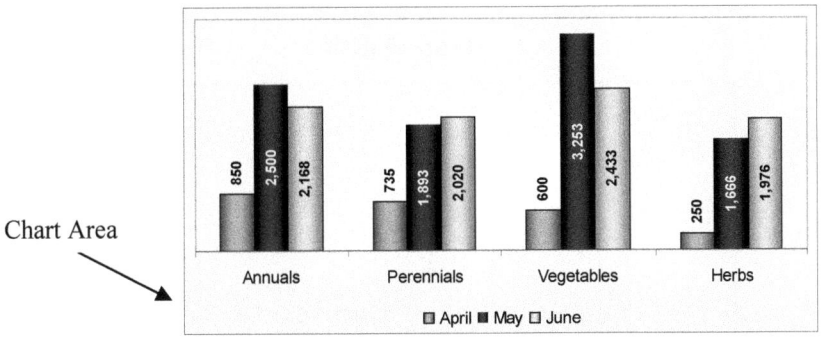

To adjust the gap width in a column chart

The gap width controls the space between the bars in a column chart.

- To adjust spacing, right-click the bar of a data series.
- Choose **Format Data Series**. Click **Series Options**
- Decrease the value of the Gap Width to reduce the space between bars.

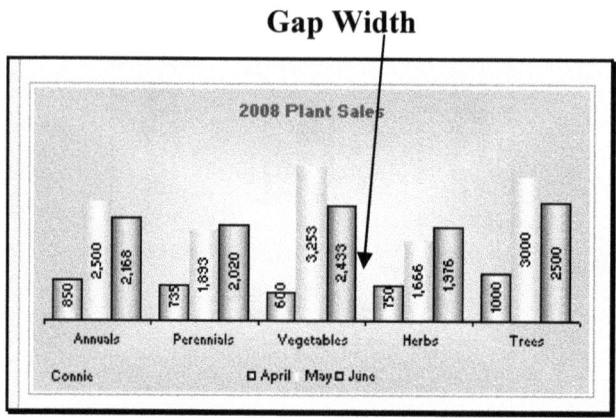

Microsoft® Excel 2007   Quick Reference Guide

To add a text note

- Select the chart and type. Click the **Layout** tab.
- Click the **Text Box** button. Click & drag on the chart where you want the text to appear. Type the text.
- To move the text box, point to the frame around the object and drag it to a new position. The mouse pointer should display a four-headed arrow before you begin dragging.
- To change its size, select it and drag an edge or corner to a new position.

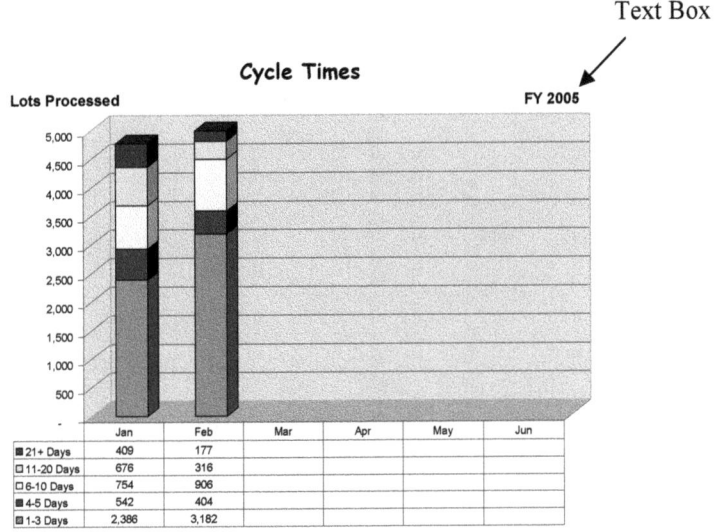

To add an Arrow or Shape

- Click to select the chart. Click the **Layout** tab.
- Click the **Shapes** button. Choose a shape.
- Click & drag on the chart where you want the shape to appear. The **Drawing Tools Format** tab displays when the shape is selected. Use the **Format** ribbon to change the appearance of the shape.

- 93 -

Microsoft® Excel 2007   Quick Reference Guide

Attaching the Data Table to a Chart

A table of the data range used to create a chart can be attached to the bottom of the chart to show the values used in the chart.

To attach the data table

- Click to select the chart.
- Click the **Layout** tab and click the **Data Table** button.
- Choose **Show Data Table** or **Show Data Table with Legend Keys**.

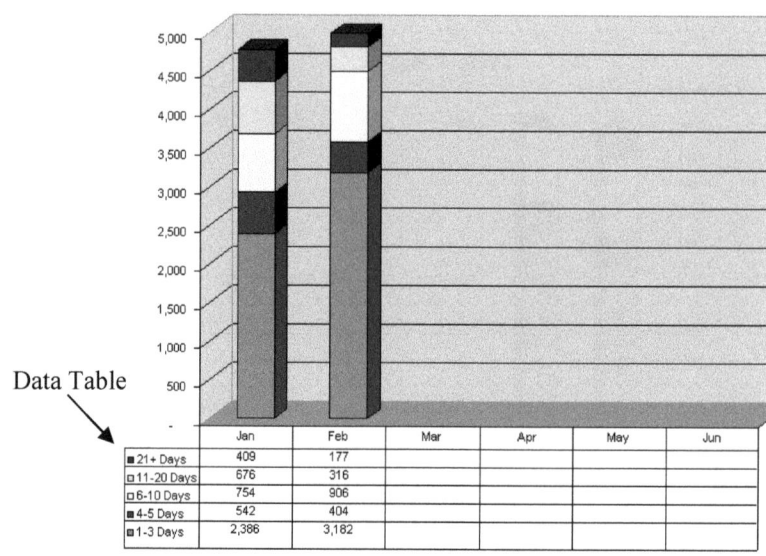

Microsoft® Excel 2007   Quick Reference Guide

Copying a Chart Sheet

To copy a chart sheet

- Hold the [CTRL] key and drag the sheet tab name.
- Release the mouse before you release the [CTRL] key.
- Rename the sheet by double-clicking on the sheet tab name, type a new name and press Enter.

To change the data range of a chart

- Click the chart area to select it. On the **Design** tab, click the **Select Data** button.

- Click the red arrow to display the chart window.
- Select the range to chart and press enter.
- ✎ To select non-adjacent ranges, drag to highlight the first range, hold the [CTRL] key and drag to select each additional range.

Templates, Tips & Timesavers

Creating a Series

Normally, the *fill handle* is used to copy data into a range. If the first value in the range is the beginning of a series, such as a date, time, month, or day of the week, Excel extends the series automatically. Excel also extends the series if the starting cell(s) include text and numbers, such as Product 1.

You can teach Excel a series by giving it the first 2 values in the series. Excel uses the difference between the values as the step value to extend the series. The values may include months, days, days of the week, quarters, years, times, or values, displayed in a variety of formats.

To create a series by dragging

- Select the first value, or the first 2 values if necessary to show the increment.

- Drag the fill handle down or to the right to extend the series to the range you want.

or Drag the fill handle up or left beyond the initial value range to extend the series by subtracting the increment.

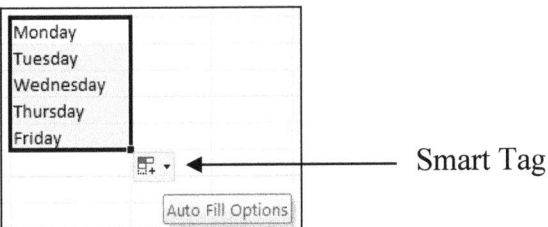

Smart Tag

✎ To force Excel to copy the initial value to a range instead of extending the series, hover over the Smart Tag and click the drop-down arrow. Choose Copy Cells.

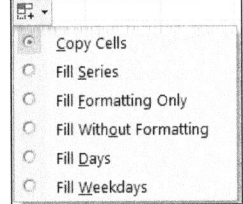

- 97 -

Microsoft® Excel 2007　　　　　Quick Reference Guide

To create a series with the Fill command

- Type the starting value(s). Select the range of cells the series should encompass, including the starting value(s).
- Click the **Home** tab. In the **Editing** group, click the **Fill** button.

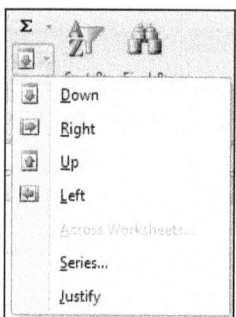

- To quick fill, choose Down, Right, Up or Left.

Or Click **Series**

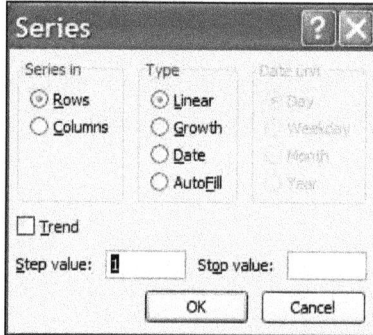

- Choose **Rows** or **Columns**
- Indicate the **Step Value** and the series **Type**.
- If the series is by **Date**, choose the **Date Unit**.
- If a **Stop Value** is given, the series stops when the value is reached even if the range is not filled.

- 98 -

Microsoft® Excel 2007   Quick Reference Guide

⏱ If you drag the fill handle using the right mouse button, a shortcut menu will display that includes fill series options.

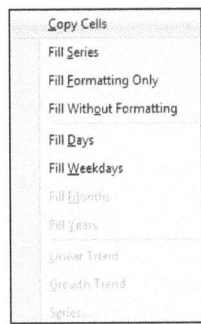

Creating Custom Lists

You can create your own Custom Lists and use the Fill Handle or Fill Series command to create a list in a worksheet.

To create your own Custom Lists

- Click the **Office Button**, and choose **Excel Options**.
- Click the **Popular** category, and then under **Top options for working with Excel**, click **Edit Custom Lists...**.
- Select **New List** from the **Custom Lists** option.
- Type the **List Entries** pressing [ENTER] after each item.
- When the list is complete, click **Add**.
- The items in the list that you selected are added to the **Custom lists** box.
- Click **OK** twice.
- Close the **Custom Lists** menu.

To use your Custom Lists

- Type the first entry for your list.
- Drag the fill handle to select the additional cells for the list. List entries are automatically filled in to the selected area.

Creating a list by importing entries

- Click the **Office Button**, and choose **Excel Options**.
- Click the **Popular** category, and then under **Top options for working with Excel**, click **Edit Custom Lists...**.

Microsoft® Excel 2007　　　Quick Reference Guide

- Type the range of cells that includes the list of entries in the **Import list from cells** text box or click the select range button to return to the spreadsheet and highlight the entries.
- Click the **Import** command button to include the entries in your custom list. Click OK.

Protecting a Workbook

To protect a worksheet with a password

- Click the Office Button .
- Highlight **Save As** and choose the file format.
- Click the **Tools** command button in the lower left of the dialogue box.
- Click **General Options**.

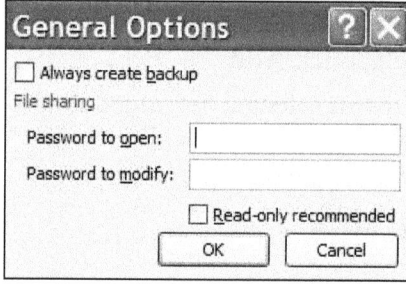

- Provide a Protection Password of up to 15 characters. Remember the password! Passwords are case-sensitive.
- Complete the process of saving the file.

Protecting cells, sheets, and workbooks from changes

All cells are locked and the worksheet protection is *disabled* when a file is first created. Before enabling the worksheet protection, unlock the cells that will receive input.

Microsoft® Excel 2007   Quick Reference Guide

- Select all cells where input will be allowed. To select non-adjacent cells, click the first cell, hold the [CTRL] key and click each additional cell.
- On the **Home** tab, click the Dialog Box Launcher next to Font group.
- Click the **Protection** folder tab. Deselect the **Lock** option.
- To enable the workbook protection, click the **Review** tab.
- Click the **Protect Sheet** button.

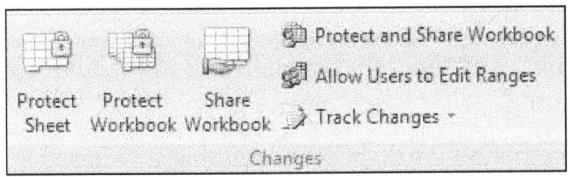

- Decide if you want to specify a password. Keep in mind the worksheet can not be unprotected if you forget the password.
- Choose the check box items that users will be allowed to change.

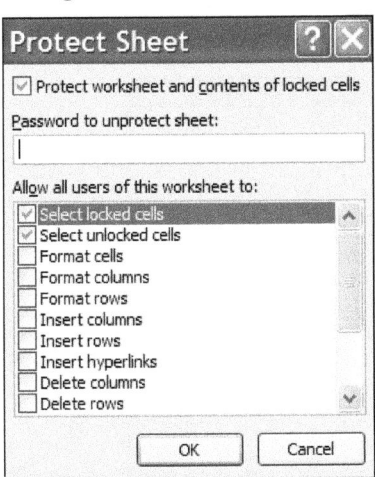

✎ When a workbook is protected the tab key will move among the unlocked cells only.

To unprotect the sheet, click the **Review** tab and choose **Unprotect Sheet.**

- 101 -

Microsoft® Excel 2007 — Quick Reference Guide

Templates

A *template* is a workbook that is used as a model for other workbooks. The template may contain formatting, formulas, text, print margins and headers, and so on. When a template is opened, Excel automatically opens a copy of the template, and leaves the original untouched so it can be used again. Templates saved in compatibility mode have the extension .XLT.

To create a template

- Create a new worksheet that contains all of the text, formulas, and formatting.

or Modify an existing worksheet by deleting unwanted information.

- Click the **Office Button**, highlight **Save As** and choose the file format you want – i.e., Excel Workbook or Excel 97-2003 Workbook. Specify a name for the template.
- Change the **Save File as Type** to **Template**.

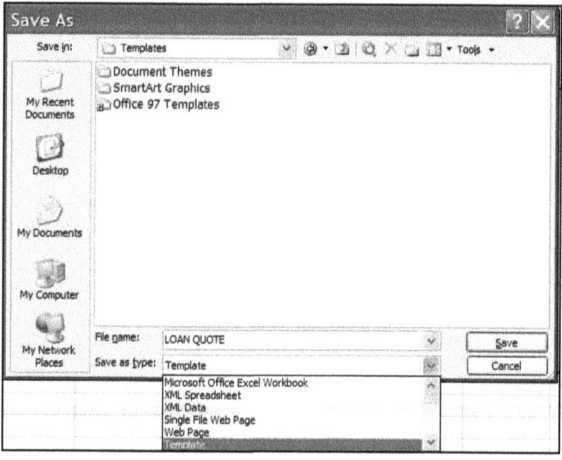

Microsoft® Excel 2007　　　　　Quick Reference Guide

To use a template

♦ Click the **Office Button** and choose **New**.

♦ Click **My Templates** on the left side of the window.

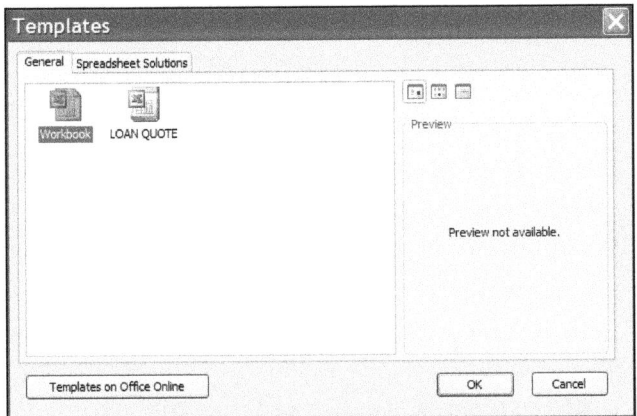

♦ Double-click the button for the name of the template.

Excel creates a copy of the template with a new name, and with the extension .XLS. You may provide a different name for the file when you save it.

To modify a template

♦ Create a new file from the existing template using the steps shown above.

♦ Modify the file as needed.

♦ Click the **Office Button**, choose **Save As** and change the **Save File as Type** to **Template**. Specify the same exact filename as the original template. You will be prompted to replace the original template. Choose YES.

✎ Changes made to the template affect future worksheets based on the template, but not worksheets that already exist.

Microsoft® Excel 2007 — Quick Reference Guide

Using Select Special

To find specific types of cells

- Move to where the search should begin, or select a range within which to search.
- Press [CTRL][G] and choose **Special**.
- Indicate the type of cell to find.

    Current Region selects the block (contiguous non-blank cells) that surrounds the current cell. [CTRL][SHIFT][*] will also find the current region (use the 8 key in conjunction with the shift key) or [CTRL] * on the numeric keypad.

    Current Array selects the array range for the current cell.

    Visible Cells Only ignores hidden cells.

    Last Cell selects the cell at the intersection of the last row and column used in the current sheet, which you can also find with [CTRL][END].

    Data Validation locates cells that includes restrictions when entering information into a cell. For example, you can set a validation rule that limits the input to a date format only.

    Choose **Constants** to find cells that have text. This is also useful to locate cells that appear to be empty but contain a space.

Microsoft® Excel 2007　　　Quick Reference Guide

Using data validation rules

* To set a data validation rule for a cell or range of cells, click the **Data** tab.
* Click the **Data Validation** button.
* On the **Settings** folder tab, click the **Allow** drop-down to specify the condition for data entry.

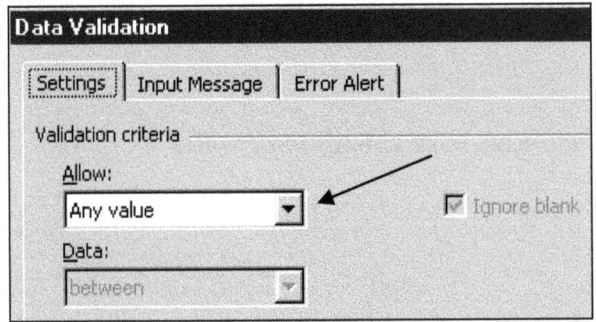

* Click the **Error Alert** folder tab. Specify a **Title** for the dialogue box and **error message** that should display when invalid data is entered.

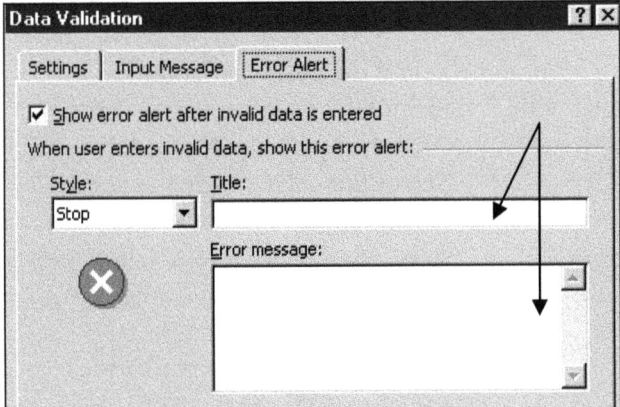

* ✎ The **Input Message** folder tab is used if you want a pop-up message to display when the user clicks on the cell that includes a data validation rule. I usually skip this option because it can be distracting.

Microsoft® Excel 2007   Quick Reference Guide

To compare 2 rows or columns

- Select cells in the rows or columns to compare.
- Press [CTRL][G], and choose **Special**.
- Choose **Row Differences** to compare values within the same row, or **Column Differences** to compare values within a column. Cells that do not match remain selected.

Cell contents must be identical to be considered the same. Formulas that result in the same value are considered different.

Replacing formulas with calculated results

copy information from above	Press [CTRL] apostrophe . If the above cell contains a formula, it is copied exactly and does not adjust the row to become relative to the new address.
replace formula with value	Select the cell, click on the formula bar, and press [F9].
replace several formulas with values	Select the cells that contain formulas you want to convert, click **Copy** on the Home tab. Select the cells where the results should appear, or leave the selected cells selected. Click the arrow on the bottom of the Paste button and choose **Paste Special**. Choose **Paste Values** and click **OK**. Press [ESC] to clear the flashing marquee.

Microsoft® Excel 2007   Quick Reference Guide

To find precedents and dependents of the current cell

Precedents are cells referred to in formulas within the selected cell. *Dependents* are cells containing formulas that refer to the selected cell.

- Click the **Formulas** tab.

- Click on a formula and use the [Trace Precedents] button to display arrows to the cells used in the calculation.

- Click on a value and use the [Trace Dependents] button to draw arrows to formulas that would change if you change the value.

Greenhouse Construction		Price Each	Projected Amount
5	40 x 100 Greenhouse Frame	950.00	4,750.00
5	Rolls 3-year plastic	299.00	1,495.00
75	Tables for plants	30.00	2,250.00
5	Furnace/heating system for each house	1,250.00	6,250.00
10	Large Exhaust fan/cooling system	325.00	3,250.00
5	Pipe for watering system/fertization	850.00	4,250.00
	Total Greenhouse Construction		$22,245.00

Microsoft® Excel 2007   Quick Reference Guide

To print formulas

When you write a formula, the result of the formula displays in the cell. If you want to display or print the actual formula:

- Hold [CRTL] and press the Grave accent key.

Formulas will display in the cells. To print you may need to adjust column width. To toggle off the display of formulas and return to formula results press [CRTL] Accent again.

Greenl		Price Each	Projected Amount
5	40 x 100 Greenhouse Frame	950	=C7*A7
5	Rolls 3-year plastic	299	=C8*A8
75	Tables for plants	30	=C9*A9
5	Furnace/heating system for each house	1250	=C10*A10
10	Large Exhaust fan/cooling system	325	=C11*A11
5	Pipe for watering system/fertization	850	=C12*A12
	Total Greenhouse Construction		=SUM(D7:D13)

Rearranging Windows

To open a second window displaying the active document

- On the **View** tab click the **New Window** button. This produces 2 views of the same document. Changes to the document in either window are reflected in both windows.
- Click **Arrange All**, then choose:

   Tiled to divide the display among all open windows by dividing the window horizontally and vertically.

   Horizontal to create multiple horizontal windows.

   Vertical to create multiple side-by-side windows.

- 108 -

Microsoft® Excel 2007   Quick Reference Guide

- When **Windows of Active Workbook** is turned on, only the windows that belong to the active workbook are rearranged.

To divide a window into panes

- On the **View** tab, click [Split]. This splits the window into 4 *panes*, using the current cell as the intersection of the split lines. If the current cell is at the top or left side of the window, only 2 panes are created.
- When the active window is split into panes, horizontally and/or vertically, scrolling is automatically synchronized in both directions. To return to a single pane, click the [Split] button again.

To freeze columns and rows

When you scroll down through a workbook, the heading rows at the top of the worksheet will not be visible and when you scroll to the right in a wide spreadsheet descriptive columns on the left will not be visible. Use Freeze panes to lock *Reference rows* and/or *columns* within a window so that they remain visible when a large document is scrolled.

- Move the cell pointer to the intersection of the first row below the reference rows and the first column to the right of the reference columns.

- On the **View** tab click the **Freeze Panes** button. Choose one of the following:

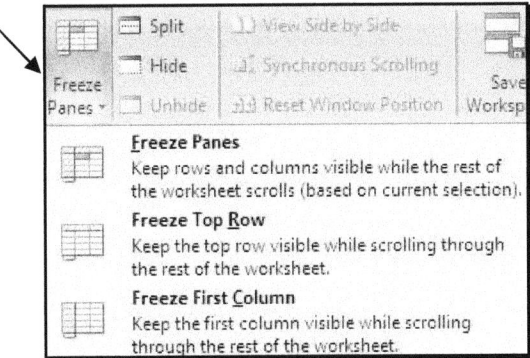

- 109 -

Microsoft® Excel 2007   Quick Reference Guide

- Scrolling now affects only the lower right quadrant of the screen.
- To remove frozen rows and columns, click **Freeze Panes** again on the View tab and choose **Unfreeze Panes**.

To print column headings at the top of every page

- Click the **Page Layout** tab on the ribbon.
- Click the **Print Titles** button.
- Specify the **Rows to repeat at top** or click the icon to select the range.

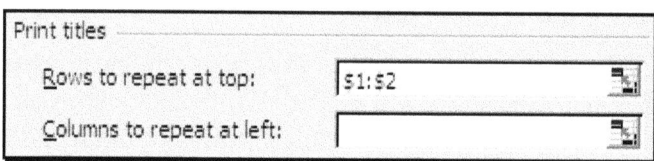

- Click OK.

- 110 -

Microsoft® Excel 2007   Quick Reference Guide

Cell Comments

A *text Comment* is a comment attached to a cell. Comments can be printed or reviewed on the screen, but they do not appear as part of the spreadsheet. With the proper recording hardware, you can record and add sound Comments to cells.

To create a comment

- Click the cell the Comment will be attached to. Click the **Review** tab.
- Click the **New Comment** button or press [SHIFT][F2].

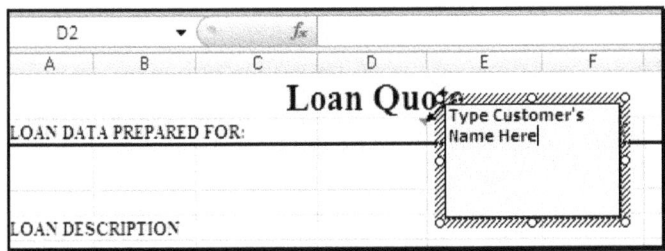

- Type the comment in the **Text Comment** box. A small dot displays in the upper right corner of cells that have Comments attached.

To delete a comment

- Select the cell that includes the comment box. On the **Review** tab, click **Delete** button in the **Comments** group.

To display comments

- Click the **Show/Hide Comment** button in the Comments group of the **Review** tab.

To print comments

- Click the **Page Layout** tab. Double-click the ▣Dialogue Box launcher. On the **Sheet** folder tab, click the comments

Microsoft® Excel 2007   Quick Reference Guide

drop down. Select **At end of sheet** or **As displayed on sheet**.

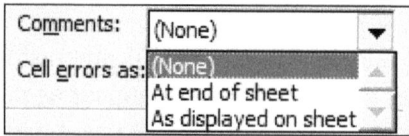

To reformat a comment box

- Click on the cell that includes the comment box. On the **Review** tab, click the **Show/Hide Comment** button.
- Position the mouse on the frame around the comment and right-click. Chose **Format Comment**. Make the format selections and click OK.

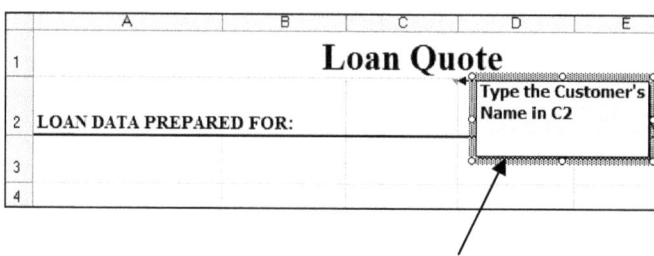

Microsoft® Excel 2007   Quick Reference Guide

Cell Styles

A *style* includes one or more of the following characteristics: number format, font, alignment, border, pattern, and protection. A style can be applied to cells and copied to other worksheets. When a style is modified, all of the cells that use it are changed automatically. By default, all cells in a sheet are set to the **Normal** style. Excel has many built in styles.

To apply a style

- Select the cell(s) to receive the style. On 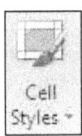 the **Home** tab, click the **Cell Styles** button.

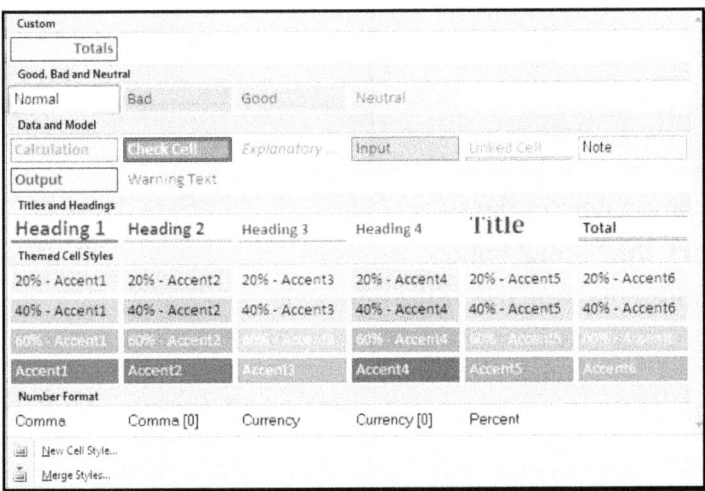

- Hover over a style to see a live preview. Click the style you want to apply.

Microsoft® Excel 2007 — Quick Reference Guide

To create a new cell style

- Select cell(s) to receive the style.
- On the **Home** tab, click the **Cell Styles** button.
- Click [New Cell Style...].

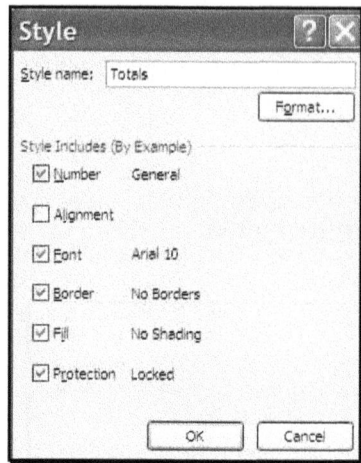

- Type a name for the style.
- Click the Format button.
- Choose the formats for the new style.
- Click OK twice.

To copy styles from another workbook

- Open the workbook that contains the styles you want to copy.
- Also open the workbook that the styles will be copied to.
- On the **Home** tab, click the **Cell Styles** button.
- Click [Merge Styles...].
- Click the name of the open file that includes the styles you want to merge. Click OK.
- To apply the merged styles, highlight the range and choose the style from the **Custom** section of the Cell Styles list.

➘ All styles in a workbook will change when you modify the style. However, styles that are merged into a different

Microsoft® Excel 2007   Quick Reference Guide

workbook and then modified will not change the styles in the original workbook.

Conditional Formatting

Conditional Formatting is used to monitor cell values or a result of a formula by defining a cell format that should be applied when a condition is met. For example, in a business plan you might create a spreadsheet that includes income projections for the upcoming year. Throughout the year you enter the actual numbers. Using conditional formatting you can format a cell that does not meet the projected amount in red or show the result in bright yellow if the actual amount exceeds your expectations.

To set conditional formatting

- Select the cell(s) that will include the conditions.
- On the **Home** tab, click the **Conditional Formatting** button in the **Styles** Group.

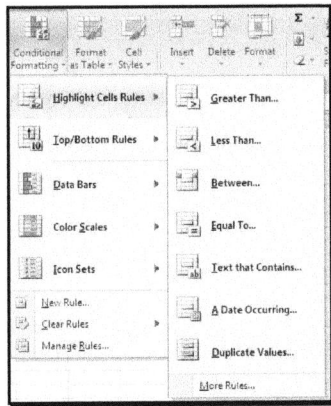

- Choose a category from the list of the left, for example **Highlight Cell Rules**.
- Choose a condition, for example **Less Than...**
- Choose a formatting option and click OK.

- 115 -

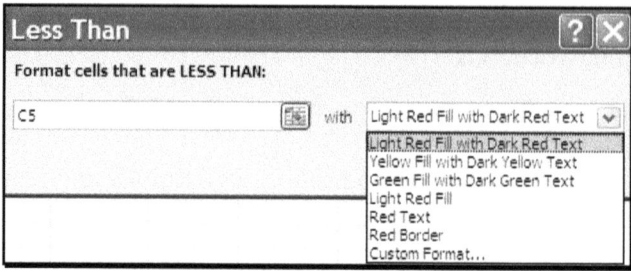

To remove conditional formatting

- Select the cell(s) that has conditions.
- On the **Home** tab, click the **Conditional Formatting** button in the **Styles** Group.
- Highlight **Clear Rules** and click **Clear Rules from Selected Cells**.

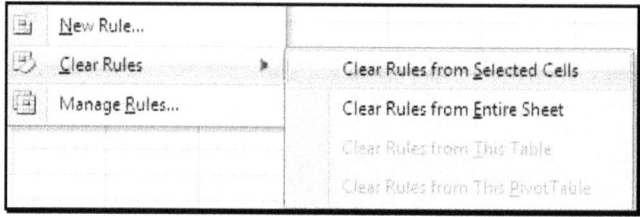

Microsoft® Excel 2007   Quick Reference Guide

Track Changes

The track changes feature is used to mark where changes have been made in a workbook. As changes are marked, a comment is created for the cell that includes who made the change, the date and what the change was.

To track changes

- On the **Review** tab, click the **Track Changes** button.

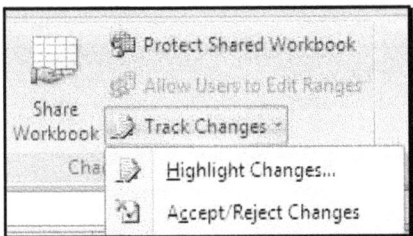

- Click **Highlight Changes** and turn on **Track Changes While Editing**.

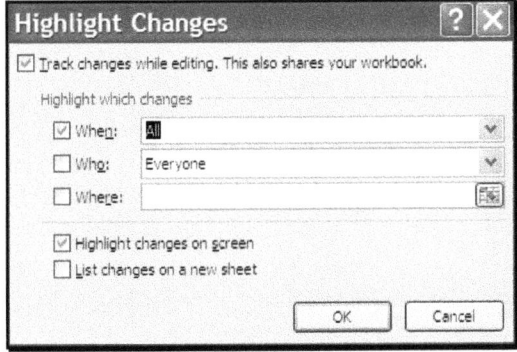

- Specify options for **When**, **Who** and **Where**. Click OK. When prompted to save, type a new filename and click OK. As changes are made, comments will be added to the cell.
- To view a change, click the cell that has a track changes marker in the upper left corner of the cell. A box will display to show changes.

- 117 -

To review changes in a document

- On the **Review** tab, click the **Track Changes** button. Choose **Accept or Reject Changes** and click OK.
- Click the **When** drop down list and choose **Since Date**. Accept the suggested date or specify a new date. Click OK.
  - **Accept All** removes the comment marker and all changes become permanent.
  - **Reject All** reverses all revisions, and removes revision markers.
  - **Accept** or **Reject** will stop at each revision until all changes have been viewed.

Databases Functions

Sorting Information

In previous versions of Excel, sort was limited to 3 levels. Excel 2007 can sort up to 64 levels. In addition to more levels, you can also sort by color. To perform a quick sort by one column:

- Select the range to sort. This should include all columns in the spreadsheet. If you select a single column, Excel will prompt to Expand the selection or Continue with the current selection.

- Press [TAB] or [ENTER] if necessary to move the current cell to the column to sort by.

- Click the **Data** tab on the ribbon and click Ascending or Descending tool.

- or On the **Data** tab, click the **Sort** button.

- Choose the first field you want to sort by.

- Click **Add Level** to add more columns to sort by.
  You can include up to 64 levels to sort by.

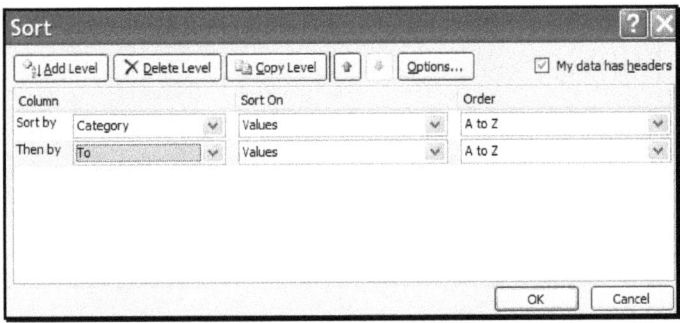

- Specify whether the selected area includes a **Header Row** or not. If so, the header row is not included in the sort.

- 119 -

Microsoft® Excel 2007   Quick Reference Guide

Pivot Tables

Pivot Tables are used to analyze and summarize lists and worksheet data. The list or database must follow the standard rules for a database:

- The row with field names must use a different format than the list. This can be as simple as a bold or center format.
- Do not include any blank rows or columns in the list. A blank cell is OK but not an entirely blank row/column.
- When working with database information, consistency is critical. If you enter the state as NH, N.H. New Hampshire or N. H. – this would be considered 4 different states when using filters to select criteria.

PivotTables are much easier to use than in earlier versions of Excel. You no longer have to drag data to drop zones, simply select the fields that you want to see in a new PivotTable field list.

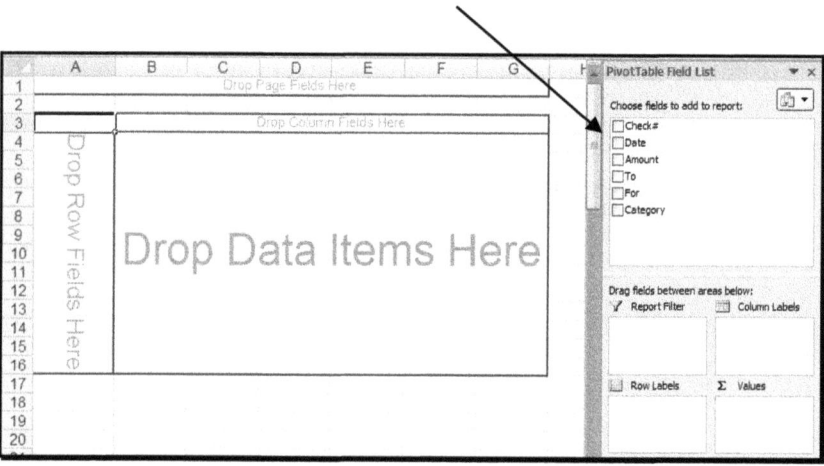

Microsoft® Excel 2007   Quick Reference Guide

To create a PivotTable

+ Click on any cell within the database list.
+ Click the **Insert** tab.
+ Click the **PivotTable** button on the ribbon.

Note: The PivotTable button has 2 parts
The top part will assume you are creating a PivotTable, whereas the bottom part will drop down choices for PivotTable or PivotChart.

+ Choose **PivotTable**.

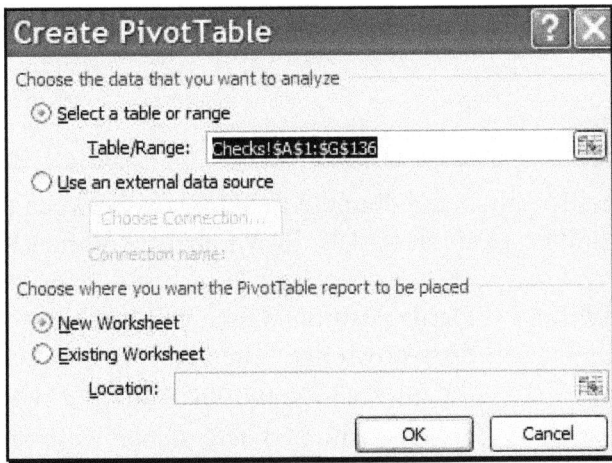

+ Confirm or change the range that contains the data or choose to Use an external data source.
+ Choose where you want the PivotTable to be placed – on a **New Worksheet** or on an **Existing Worksheet**. Click OK.
+ The **PivotTable Tools** tab is added to the ribbon and includes the **Options** and **Design** tab.

Microsoft® Excel 2007　　Quick Reference Guide

- Choose the fields to add to the PivotTable by clicking the field check boxes.

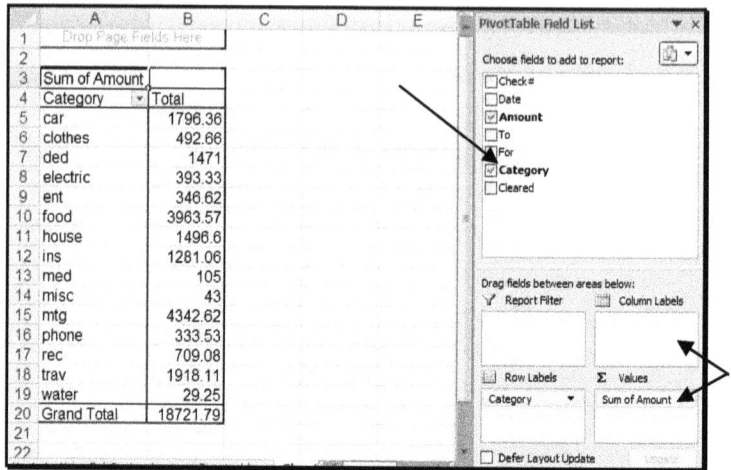

- If necessary, click and drag the field buttons between the Report Filter, Column Labels, Row Labels or Values boxes

Report Filter	Fields positioned here will be shown with a drop-down list. The PivotTable summarizes the information for one value at a time.
Row Labels	Fields positioned here display with one value per row in the resulting PivotTable.
Column Labels	Fields here display with one value per column in the resulting PivotTable.
Values	Fields here are summarized, normally with a total.

Microsoft® Excel 2007   Quick Reference Guide

Grouping Categories and Show/Hide Details

When categories in a PivotTable have been grouped together, the **Expand & Collapse Entire Field** feature can be used display totals for items in the group.

Sample without grouping: **Sample with grouping:**

Sum of Amount	
Category	Total
car	$1,796.36
clothes	$492.66
ded	$1,471.00
ent	$346.62
food	$3,963.57
house	$1,496.60
ins	$1,281.06
med	$105.00
misc	$43.00
mtg	$4,342.62
rec	$709.08
trav	$1,918.11
util	$756.11
Grand Total	$18,721.79

Sum of Amount		
Grouped	Category	Total
Miscellaneous	car	$1,796.36
	ded	$1,471.00
	misc	$43.00
	util	$756.11
Personal	clothes	$492.66
	food	$3,963.57
	med	$105.00
Entertainment	ent	$346.62
	rec	$709.08
	trav	$1,918.11
Household	house	$1,496.60
	ins	$1,281.06
	mtg	$4,342.62
Grand Total		$18,721.79

To group categories

- Click the first category name (example, car)
- Hold the [CTRL] key and click each additional category name (example ded, misc, util)
- Right-click on one of the selected categories.
- Click **Group**. A general name is assigned to the group, i.e., Group1, Group2, etc.
- Click on the cell that contains the group name and type a new name for the group. Press Enter.

Microsoft® Excel 2007 — Quick Reference Guide

Expanding & Collapsing the Details

When categories have been grouped together, using Collapse Entire Group will display the main category only with a total for the grouped items. When you Expand Entire Field, the amount for each category will display and you do not see a total for the grouped items.

Grouped with details showing:

Sum of Amount		
Grouped ▼	Category ▼	Total
Miscellaneous	car	$1,796.36
	ded	$1,471.00
	misc	$43.00
	util	$756.11
Personal	clothes	$492.66
	food	$3,963.57
	med	$105.00
Entertainment	ent	$346.62
	rec	$709.08
	trav	$1,918.11
Household	house	$1,496.60
	ins	$1,281.06
	mtg	$4,342.62
Grand Total		$18,721.79

Grouped using Collapse:

Sum of Amount		
Grouped ▼	Category ▼	Total
Miscellaneous		$4,066.47
Personal		$4,561.23
Entertainment		$2,973.81
Household		$7,120.28
Grand Total		**$18,721.79**

To collapse category details

- Click an individual category name or drag to select a range of categories.
- Click the [Collapse Entire Field] on the **PivotTable Tools Options** tab on the ribbon.
- To redisplay the details, highlight cells and click the [Expand Entire Field] on the **PivotTable Tools Options** tab on the ribbon.

Microsoft® Excel 2007 — Quick Reference Guide

Updating PivotTable Data

- If you edit data in a database list that you have used to create a pivot table, you should refresh the Pivot Table to ensure that all of the information has been updated.
- To update a pivot table, click somewhere in the Pivot Table.
- Click the **Refresh** button on the PivotTable Tool Options tab on the ribbon.

PivotTable Formatting Styles

The PivotTable Tools Design tab on the ribbon is used to quickly apply different styles to enhance the appearance of the PivotTable report.

To apply a design

- Click on a cell in the PivotTable.
- Click the **PivotTable Tools Design** tab on the ribbon.
- Click a PivotTable Style.

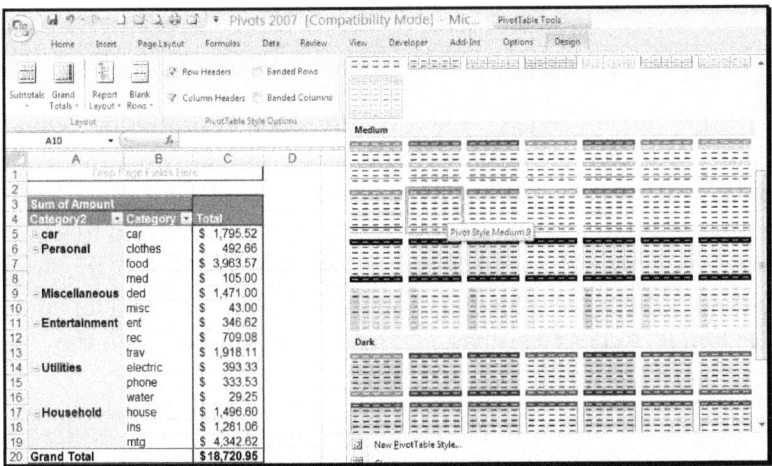

- 125 -

Microsoft® Excel 2007   Quick Reference Guide

Using a List as a Database

Excel can view any list as a *database*, where rows are *records* and columns are *fields*.

To use a list as a database

- If possible, place the list on its own sheet.
- Create column labels (field names) in the first row of the list. Format them differently than the data in the list, so that they are more easily identified as column labels.
- Name the list if desired. If the name Database is used, Excel assumes the first row contains field names. It also assumes this if the first row is formatted differently.
- Do not include any blank rows or columns in the list. A blank cell is OK but not an entire blank row/column.
- When working with database information, consistency is critical. If you enter the state as NH, N.H. New Hampshire or N. H. – this would be considered 4 different states when using filters to select criteria.

Using the data form

The *data form* is a dialog box used to look at or modify one database record at a time. This is a convenient way to view the data, rather than scrolling from left to right to view all information in a row. The data form can also be used to search for records based on common criteria. In Excel 2007, the Form button has not been included on the Ribbon, but you can add it to the Quick Access Toolbar. To add the Form button to the toolbar:

- Click the arrow at the end of the **Quick Access Toolbar**, and then click **More Commands**.
- In the Choose commands from box, click **All Commands**.
- In the list box, highlight **Form** and click **Add**.

Microsoft® Excel 2007 Quick Reference Guide

- To display a data form, click anywhere in the database list and click the new **Form** button on the toolbar.

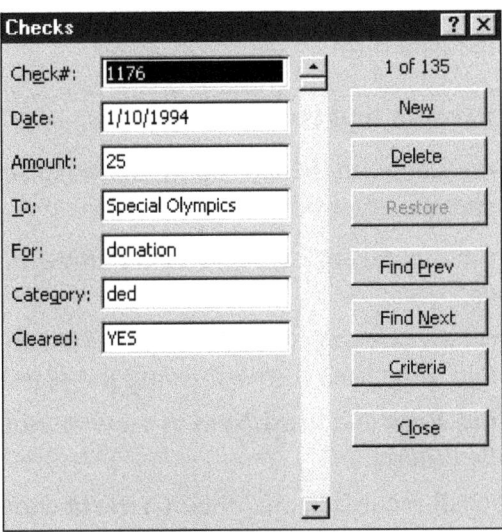

- The sheet tab name displays on the title bar of the data form. The field names appear on the left, with text boxes to their right. Protected fields, and calculated fields which result from formulas, cannot be edited and do not appear in text boxes.
- The record number and total number of records appear in the upper right corner. Use the scroll bar to find the record you want, or use **Find Prev** and **Find Next** to locate a record.
- Press [TAB] to move from one field to another or use the mouse to click in the text box.
- To change information in a field, highlight if necessary and retype to edit the entry. The **Restore** button is used to remove all changes to the record currently displayed. Changes are reflected in the sheet list when you go to a different record.
- Choose **Delete** to remove the current record from the database. Deletions are permanent.
- To add a new record to the end of the list, click the **New** command button and type into the text boxes, pressing [TAB]

to move from field to field. Press [ENTER] to complete the record and begin a new one.

List information can also be changed in sheet cells, without using the data form.

To use criteria to find records

The *Criteria* feature in the data form is used to search for records that meet specific conditions.

- In the data form, click the **Criteria** button. A blank form displays.
- Type values or expressions (such as *>100* or *<=1/1/08*) into each field to be used for performing the search criteria.
- Use **Find Prev** and **Find Next** to view all of the records that meet the criteria.
- To view all records again, click **Criteria** choose **Clear**, then **Form**.

Microsoft® Excel 2007   Quick Reference Guide

Filtering Records

A *filter* hides all records that do not meet criteria, and displays only records that do. When you use the Filter feature drop-down arrows display to the right of each field name. When you click the drop-down, a list of all the unique entries displays to enable quick filtering. Filters can be applied to multiple fields.

In Excel 2007 the Filter feature has been expanded to include filtering by color, selecting multiple items to filter and filter by date.

To turn on the Filter Feature

- Click on any cell within the database list, or select multiple contiguous column headers to show filter criteria only for specific columns.
- Click the **Data** tab on the ribbon,
- Click the **Filter** button. A list box of unique values can be opened under each column header.
- Select values in one or more columns to hide all records that do not match. When a filter is in use, a small filter symbol displays to the right of the column heading.
- To remove the filter and show all records, click the button to the right of the column heading and click **Select All**.
- To turn off the Filter feature and remove the drop-down arrows, click the **Data** tab on the ribbon and click the **Filter** button.
- A filtered list can be formatted, copied, printed, edited, sorted, charted, or autosummed. When any of these features are used, hidden records are not affected.

Microsoft® Excel 2007   Quick Reference Guide

Calculating in a Database

When working with a database you may want to calculate a subtotal, average, perform a count, display a high or low value or perform other simple functions. Using the **Data Subtotal** feature, calculations can be inserted automatically at each change in a category and later removed to return to the standard database format.

To calculate automatic subtotals and totals in a database

Sort the list by the column that should be subtotaled, so that all records to be included in a single subtotal are grouped together.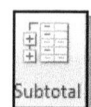

- Click the **Data** tab on the ribbon.
- Click the **Subtotals** button.

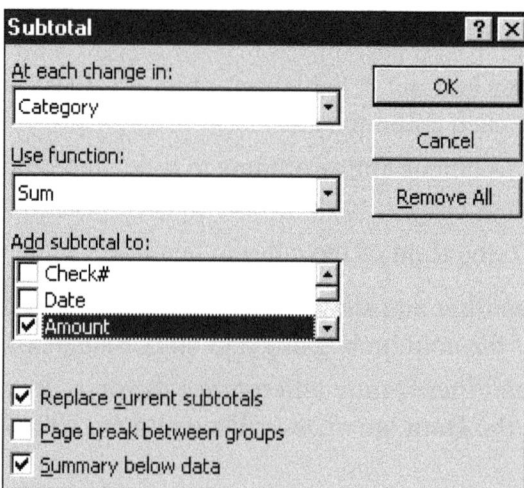

- Set **At Each Change in** to the column the records are sorted by.
- Set **Use Function** to one of the summary calculations.
- Turn on all fields in **Add Subtotal to** that should display a subtotal.
- To force a page break after each group, turn on **Page Break Between Groups**.

- To display summary calculations above each group instead of below, turn off **Summary Below Data**.

    When the summary calculations appear, outline symbols and level bars are added.

    To print or chart subtotals only, hide lower outline levels.

    To display summary calculations for part of a list, filter the list first.

    To display more than one summary calculation for each group, such as **Sum** and **Average**, define one set of calculations, then return to **Data Subtotals**, turn off **Replace Current Subtotals**, and define additional summary calculations.

    To nest groups, providing subtotals within subtotals, start with a multi-level sort. Use **Data Subtotals** to provide subtotals for one grouping level. Return to **Data Subtotals**, turn off **Replace Current Subtotals**, and define the subtotals for the other grouping level.

    To remove all summary calculations, choose **Data Subtotals Remove All**.

Microsoft® Excel 2007   Quick Reference Guide

Database Functions

Purpose: Database functions perform calculations (sum, count, average, etc.) on a subset of a database defined by a criterion range.

Format:
=DSUM(database,field#,criteria)
=DAVERAGE(database,field#,criteria)
=DCOUNT(database,field#,criteria)
=DMAX(database,field#,criteria)

Arguments:

database — range of cells, or a defined name, that defines the database. The top row must include column headings or field names.

field — sequence number of the field, starting with 1, or the field name, in double quotes " ", of the field to be summarized.

criteria — range of cells, or a defined name, that contains database criteria.

Examples:
=DCOUNT(employees,2,criteria)
=DSUM(employees,"Salary",criteria)
=DMAX(employees,"HireDate",criteria).

	A	B	C	D	E	F
1	Check#	Date	To	For	Amount	Category
2						
3						
4						
5						
6						
7						
8						
9	Total Amount of Checks		=DSUM(Checks,"amount",A1:F2)			
10	Average Check Amount		=DAVERAGE(Checks,"amount",A1:F2)			
11	Total # of Checks Written		=DCOUNT(Checks,"amount",A1:F2)			

Microsoft® Excel 2007   Quick Reference Guide

To define a criterion range

A *criterion range* includes one or more columns and two or more rows. The top row must contain field names that match field names (column headings) in the database. Cells below the top row contain values, comparison expressions, and/or wildcard characters to limit which records in the database qualify.

For *wildcard characters* in text, use **?** to specify a single character, or ***** to specify 1 or more characters. Excel assumes each value ends with *****.

Examples:

Smith	starting with Smith
=Smith	exact match
<100	less than 100
>=1/1/08	on or after 1/1/08
*Associates	ending with Associates
p?ne	any character in 2nd position: pane, Pine, p2Ne
<>NY	any value except NY

Microsoft® Excel 2007   Quick Reference Guide

Index

Cell
    Comments 111
    Styles 113

Center page 33

Charts
    Add arrow or shape 93
    Axis titles 86
    Change to chart sheet 78
    Chart area 91
    Copy sheet 95
    Creating 77
    Customize data bars 87
    Customizing 85
    Data table 94
    Edit data 82
    Edit range 95
    Editing 81
    Gap width 92
    Gridlines 90
    Layout 85
    Legend 87
    Move or resize 80
    Multiple ranges 82
    Plot area 90
    Scale 89
    Show values 90
    Text note 93

Column
    Adjust width in print preview 17
    Autofit 16
    Freeze headings 48
    Hide 18
    Unhide 19
    Width 16

Compare rows or columns 106

Conditional formatting 115

Copy
    Between files 31
    Between sheets 30
    Cells 6, 29
    Formulas 15, 30
    From above cell 30
    Values 30

Create
    New file 8
    Series 15

Data
    Validation Rules 105

Database
    Autofilter 129
    Calculating 130
    Criteria 128
    Data form 126
    Filter records 129
    Functions 132
    Subtotals 130

Database Features 126

Date
    Automatic Update 6
    Format 7
    Shortcut 6

Delete
    Cell contents 13
    Cell contents & formatting 13
    Cell Format 13
    Rows or columns 27

Edit
    Data 4

Fill
    Series 14, 98
    Series, custom lists 99

Fit page 34

Font
    Changing size and style 37

Format
    Alignment 42
    Bold, italics, underline 37
    Borders 38
    Cell shading 38
    Center across cells 44
    Columns 16
    Conditional format 115
    Copy format 47
    Custom formats 41

- i -

Microsoft® Excel 2007 — Quick Reference Guide

Decimal places 39
Font color 38
Merge cells 44
Numbers 39
Numbers with $ 39
Rotate text 43
Text 37, 42
Wrap text 43

Formula Bar 2

Formulas
   Absolute referencing 54
   Add columns or rows 53
   Auditing 68
   AutoSum 53
   AVERAGE 56
   COUNT 57
   COUNTA 57
   COUNTBLANK 57
   Creating 51
   Current Date 6
   DAVERAGE 132
   DCOUNT 132
   DMAX 132
   DSUM 132
   Functions 57
   HLOOKUP 63
   IF Statement 61
   Link to other sheets 74
   Link to other workbooks 75
   MAX 56
   MIN 56
   NOW 7
   Paste Function 56
   Paste functions 53
   PMT 57, 59
   Print 108
   Replace with value 106
   ROUND 60
   ROUNDDOWN 60
   ROUNDUP 60
   Special functions 51, 52
   SUM 56
   TODAY 6
   Trace dependents 68
   Trace precedents 68
   VLOOKUP 63
   Working with text 64

Frame 2
Freeze columns or rows 109

Graphs
   See charts 77

Headers & Footers 36

Insert
   Columns 26
   Rows 26

Margins 33

Move
   Around workbook 20
   Cells 28
   Drag and Drop 29

Multiple Sheets 71

Open
   File 10
   Multiple files 12

Page break
   Manual 49
   Previewing and adjusting 25
   Remove 49

Page Breaks 48

Page setup 33

Pivot Tables 120

Print
   Column headings 35, 110
   Formula 108
   Gridlines 35
   Landscape 34
   Preview 22
   Selected cells 23
   Set print area 24
   Sheet 23
   Titles on every page 36

Protect Workbook 100

Range Names 65

Recent File List 11
   Change # of files listed 11
   Pin to menu 11

Microsoft® Excel 2007   Quick Reference Guide

Save
    To 97-2003 Format 10
    Workbook 8
Screen Layout 2
Select
    Cells 21
    Range of cells 38
Series 97
Sheet
    Also see Worksheet 71
Sheet tabs 3
Sorting 119
Switch
    Between files 12
Templates 102
    Create 102
    Modify 103
Toolbars
    Customize 2

Trace precedents or dependents 107
Track Changes 117
Undo last action 13
Workbook
    Maximum Size 4
    Protection 100
Workbook Structure 4
Worksheet
    Change tab color 73
    Delete 73
    Grouping 71
    Insert 73
    Move or copy 72
    Multiple windows 108
    Rename 71
    Split panes 109
    View multiple sheets 73
Zoom 19

www.ingramcontent.com/pod-product-compliance
Ingram Content Group UK Ltd.
Pitfield, Milton Keynes, MK11 3LW, UK
UKHW022232230426
12048UKWH00016BA/1200